D1094541

My Life
As a Woman Composer

Emma Lou Diemer

The Ardent Writer Press
Brownsboro, Alabama

Visit Emma Lou Diemer's Author Page at
www.ArdentWriterPress.com

For general information about publishing with The Ardent
Writer Press contact *steve@ardentwriterpress.com* or
forward mail to:

The Ardent Writer Press,
Box 25
Brownsboro, Alabama 35741

Library of Congress Cataloging-in-Publication Data

My Life as a Woman Composer by Emma Lou Diemer

p. cm.-(Ardent Writer Press-2021) ISBN 978-1-64066-126-4 (pbk.); 978-1-64066-127-1 (hardcover) 978-1-64066-128-8 (eBook)

Library of Congress Control Number 2021945405

Library of Congress Subject Headings
*   BIOGRAPHY & AUTOBIOGRAPHY / Personal Memoirs.
*   BIOGRAPHY & AUTOBIOGRAPHY / Women
*   Music--Bio-bibliography.
*   Music--United States--20th century--Bio-bibliography
*   Music--United States--Bio-bibliography

BISAC Subject Headings
*   BIO004000   BIOGRAPHY & AUTOBIOGRAPHY / Music
*   BIO026000   BIOGRAPHY & AUTOBIOGRAPHY / Personal Memoirs
*   BIO022000   BIOGRAPHY & AUTOBIOGRAPHY / Women
*   MUS007000   MUSIC / Instruction & Study / Composition

Contents

Acknowledgments   xii

Author's Word   xiv

Dedication   xvi

Section One — Family

About Selmo Park—Our Life There   1

My Mother—Myrtle Casebolt Diemer   8

My Father—George Willis Diemer   18

Grandmothers   26

My Sister—Dorothy Diemer Hendry   34

Dorothy—Last Years   44

Dorothy and Her Poetry   52

My Brothers—George and John Diemer   56

Lois Wenger Diemer   64

Wickliffe Byron Hendry   72

Another Family   80

Marilyn MacKenzie Skiöld   84

Donald Elmo Wilson   92

Emma King and Cemeteries   98

The Sun and Families   102

The Trumpet Sounds Within My Soul   105

Section Two — Becoming a Composer and Teacher

Childhood and Playing For Church   112

My First Piano Teacher—Mrs. Payton   116

Edna Billings and the Navy   119

Teachers   122

A Freshman at the Eastman School of Music   127

Going to Music School   130

Eastman as a Freshman and Howard Hanson   133

Warrensburg and Deciding on Yale   137

Yale and Paul Hindemith   140

More About Studying at Yale   143

Music Written at Yale   148

After Yale, Fulbright in Belgium   152

Tacoma   156

Tanglewood   158

Kansas City and the Death of My Father   163

Returning to Eastman for a Ph.D.   166

Composer in the Arlington, Virginia Schools   170

Section Two — Becoming a Composer and Teacher (Continued)

My Time in Arlington and D.C.
While Composing   175

Teaching in Arlington   179

Organist for Reformation Lutheran and Music for
Kindler Commission   182

My Time with the University of Maryland   185

Moving to California to Teach at UCSB   189

Karl Geiringer and Other Faculty at UCSB   194

Life in Santa Barbara and UCSB   194

Counterpoint, Teaching at UCSB,
and the Electronic Studio   200

Last Years Of Teaching at UCSB   204

Section Three — Composing and for Whom

Big Works   210

The Concerto and I   215

Simple Songs   218

A Bit About Songs   221

Writing Easy Piano Pieces   224

Two People I wrote a Lot of Music for   228

Toccata for Piano and Nozomi Takahashi   236

The Women's Philharmonic and Music By Women   240

Ruminations on Composing   244

Homages Schomages   246

Section Four — Performing and Recording

Recital at Saint Mary's in San Francisco   254

Recital in Rome   258

Recording in London, Prague, and Bratislava   262

The Last Places I Played   266

Section Five — Churches and I

Practicing the Organ at Washington National
Cathedral   274

First Presbyterian and Church Organ Jobs   278

Candles, People, and Institutions   285

Section Six — Observations, Unique Musical Entities and Happenings

My 1912 Steinway and a Doctor   290

A Shining Light in Warrensburg, Missouri   292

Bells   294

Boys Named Billy and Bill
and a Musical Instrument   298

The Essig Collection and the Theremin   302

Pianos   306

When Practicing in Church can be Scary   312

Section Seven — More About Music

Alice Meynell   318

Creativity   318

Composing Music   324

Delaying Tactics in Music Writing   330

Electronic Music   332

Favorite Medium   334

Improvising   337

Librarians and Prokofiev   339

Occasional Music   342

Quality vs. Quantity   346

Organ Music and Organists   348

Sentimentality   352

Setting Poetry to Music   354

Toccata by Aram Khachaturian   358

Writing Away from the Keyboard   364

Section Eight — Not Necessarily About Music

The Lily Pool   370

Rowing in Eden   373

The Cleanliness of Keyboard Keys   376

Earthquake 378

Fires 380

Heights 383

Easter Sunday 2020 384

Up Early During the Pandemic 386

Glimpses 388

The Mystical Number Eleven 390

Do You Pray? 392

We Gather Together 394

Section Nine—Animals and Cars I Have Known

Dewdrop 398

Cats and Dogs 402

Old Dogs 406

Distractions 410

Cars 414

Finale — Those to Follow 418

Other Images of Family, Friends and Colleagues 426

About the Author 438

ACKNOWLEDGMENTS

This book captures my thoughts about the influences and influencers in my life and career. As you read it, you quickly understand that my family has played a large part in enabling my love of music and the lifetime and friends bound by that path, musicologists or not.

I do not profess to be a Hemingway or a Virginia Woolf, but I felt it important to reflect and I hope, you the reader, enjoy my introspection along with the images of friends (both human and otherwise!) and family that have helped me enjoy my journey.

For this book I want to thank my nephew-in-law, Steve Gierhart, publisher of the Ardent Writer Press, who helped bring some zing to stories and shape it with a beautiful layout using my life's work in text and photo. I also want to thank his wife and my niece, Bonny Pfitzer-Gierhart, for her support and editing along with similar support from another niece, Betty Augsburger and her husband Larry, whose dedication to preserving our families' images through the years and an ever-changing technology was essential.

In some of the photos there are paintings by Ann Skiöld, the daughter of Marilyn MacKenzie Skiöld. They "happened" to be in many of the photos, especially those in the vicinity of the piano downstairs and the clavinova upstairs in the house I share with Marilyn. Ann is an arts librarian at Syracuse University and spent several years working in Santa Barbara and going to school at the University of California in that city. So I thank Ann, too.

And to my too numerous to count friends and colleagues in music and education, thank you! I am so proud to be a part of this large family and group of comrades on my journey. Many have passed yet still influence my everyday life. God Bless one and all because the views have been fantastic, no matter where I have been led.

AUTHOR'S WORD

These stories, this book at least, had its beginning during the pandemic of 2020 and stretched a bit into 2021 (although technically some of my stories were written years ago when I felt compelled to write down an event or thought on music while it flitted through my mind). My original impulse, idea, was to write about my life as a composer—a woman composer, as you have noted.

This is what I began to do, but I soon found other topics in and outside music to write about, and as these developed—often during the night hours when many of us found sleep difficult during 2020 and beyond—I began to put some of them on *Facebook* mainly to have someplace to put them but also to see what reactions various readers might have.

Some writers, composers, artists have written about their own lives, but many others had no time to do this. There are a few autobiographies/personal histories by composers, but have you read any by Domenico Scarlatti? or Haydn? or Clara Schumann?

Also, many composers do not live long enough to spend time on any writing beyond music composition. I have been graced with a long life, the longest so far in my family. And after many years of productive composing (I'm one of those disgustingly prolific composers who like any excuse to write more pieces, notes, words even) it is time to tell the truth about my life and some of the music, its performers, my colleagues, professors, influences.

You may be disappointed not to find diatribes, exposés, true confessions in these stories. I am basically a joyful composer. Sometimes in writing I am so pleased with the music that is developing that I get up and run around the house (not so much any more at my age, but an enlightening image). Or, on occasion, I weep with the music I'm writing, or the words. And I am a person of great reserve. I guess that is why I write music?

I could write another book about the slights, failures, hurts. But why, really?

The depths of despair expressed musically are not for me. Sadness, yes. But not despair.

Sorry, academics, seekers of angst. (I am from Missouri.)

So read on, and enjoy the images of actual people and bits of the actual music. It's all true!

I dedicate this memoir to my father, George Willis Diemer, and my mother, Myrtle Casebolt Diemer, who started me on this path and sustained me whether I was happy or sad.

SECTION ONE
Family

Selmo Park, the President's home, and our family's home while my
father, George Diemer, was President of Central Missouri State College
from 1937-1956. Now known as the University of Central Missouri, the
college is located in Warrensburg. Selmo Park was built in 1866 and the
Diemers has extensive renovations done in 1951. Due to the extensive
need for further repairs, Selmo Park was demolished in 2015.

A view of the back of Selmo Park during our stay (top) and another view of the stately home from the front, opposite side (bottom).

The beauty of winter surrounds the President's home.

Yeater stands amidst ice and snow.

177

Selmo Park in the Winter (top). From a University of Central Missouri Yearbook in the 1960s when the school was known as Central Missouri State College. Yeater Hall is pictured below.

Selmo Park's driveway and a view from the street (top) and my mother, Myrtle Diemer, sitting in the library of the home (below).

Our family on the stairway of Selmo Park (1937) with "Orchid Girl" statue in background. George and Myrtle Diemer at top. Emma Lou and sister Dorothy Diemer (below left) and brothers George above and John below along the wall

(Above) The interior music room of Selmo Park where young ELD practiced piano on their Vose on her way to a life as a composer. Dining room at the top. (Right) A teenage Emma Lou Diemer with her dog Mickey in the gardens of Selmo Park (c 1940).

Myrtle Casebolt Diemer (1961)

My Mother
Myrtle Casebolt Diemer

"All that I am, or hope to be, I owe to my angel mother." Our greatest president wrote that. It is of course not entirely true, for me. For one thing, my mother was not always an angel (thank goodness). She had spunk and spirit and could be a fiery presence when we willful children finally "got her goat", so to speak. But, even though we were (I was) sulking in some corner upstairs after a scolding, she was soon calling to us, asking where we were, and was back to her cheerful, light-hearted self, hoping that we would return, too, and be whole again, and be a better child.

There was not much depression in my family — sadness sometimes, surely, and sometimes anger, and sometimes my father took a walk by himself after dinner to think after an especially tiring day. We were too busy to linger for long in a dark room.

When I came home from school, she always had a happy occurrence to relate. I think I enjoyed hearing my mother talk more than almost anyone else. She loved people, nearly all people. She wrote hundreds of letters. I have many of them that she wrote to me when I was away. They are housed in my papers at the university, and I must have them brought out, to hear her voice again. She had envelopes addressed to the persons she was going to write to next in her friendly, open script.

Have you ever thought how different the handwriting is of each of your family members? A study in itself. I have a niece whose handwriting is very similar to my mother's. It so happened that she, Bonny, as a child spent hours with her grandmother while her mother (my sister) was teaching. They had "school", went shopping, were great friends. Bonny told me that when she was in college, she felt as though her grandmother were watching over her, keeping her safe. There is that angel component!

My mother did not like clutter. Our house was something of a public entity, belonging not to us but to the state, and there were frequent visitors. We were expected to keep things neat. I remember that once I had too much music spread out on the piano and my mother came and with one swoop brushed it all to the floor.

We are so close to our mothers it is hard to write about them, so close in remembering them.

Myrtle (actually Suzie Myrtle — that penchant in the era for giving girls and even boys double names) Susie Myrtle Casebolt. She had a brother five years younger named Eugene. He and my mother and father and my two brothers and my sister all graduated from the college in Warrensburg, now University of Central Missouri. She, like my father, taught school at a very young age, 15-16, classes of 40 or 50 or more children in DeWitt, Missouri.

After she graduated from college she continued to teach. She also acted in local plays and it was in one of them, I believe it was the melodrama *East Lynne*, that my father saw her on stage and told his friend that she was the woman he would marry.

My mother had signed up to be a missionary to China, part of the Protestant movement at that time, intent on spreading the Christian gospel to all the world.

Fortunately, my mother chose to marry my father instead. She told me that when he proposed, his face was so pale that she could not bear to say no.

With her marriage she embarked on a life defined by her husband's. He was a college president in Kansas City (KC) and my mother delighted in the busy years of involvement in church, school, civic affairs, and a wide

My mother in 1896 with younger brother Eugene

My mother's brother, Eugene c. 1937

variety of people who were dinner guests from time to time.

At the college there were learned faculty, including Emma Serl who taught English and was the author of a number of children's books. You can "google" her. My mother named me after Miss Serl and also after Lou Commack, another cherished friend, whose husband was a superintendent of schools.

My mother had a number of very close friends, and I remember that one of them, Lida Seamans, was so devoted to her that Lida brought a pie all the way across town, riding on the bus, to bring it to her. (My mother thought that was a little over the top; do you remember your mother's reaction to so many, many incidents?).

Some days my mother took the streetcar to downtown Kansas City and shopped, occasionally taking in a movie. I'm sure she was happy to sometimes escape her bustling family. When she came home in the late afternoon, I can remember myself, a child, rushing to the door to greet her, probably sobbing a bit because she had been gone so long.

She knew the saleswomen in the downtown stores; they saved items that were going on sale, saved them for when she came in again.

My mother liked all kinds of foods and we took the elevator to the tea room in Emery Bird Thayer department store, to have a treat, and a cafeteria in the Country Club Plaza (a magical place still, designed by J.C. Nichols) where we would have lunch.

Nichols, by the way, went to the same church that we did: Country Club Christian. Or it may have been J.C. Penney; one of them belonged to that church and sat in a pew near us. The minister, a rather old and grandfatherly man, was a favorite of my parents, and his wife was the organist, a position that my mother hoped I would have some day — not to be, not there.

When we moved from KC to Warrensburg, where again my mother was "the president's wife", there was a change in her "duties". She was an expert in planning receptions and teas for the students and faculty and was the best arranger of flowers that I knew. And she was active in our church, reorganizing the church school at one point. But I, in later years when I had a little more knowledge, wondered if she missed the bigger city. We drove there frequently — only 50 miles away.

My grandmother lived with us — I've written about her earlier and Dorothy wrote a book about her life — and she had a house across the campus that she rented to faculty members sometimes and could retreat to when there was any slight and harmless tension between her and my mother.

My grandmother had a Steinway upright piano, a lovely instrument, new and resonant. There seems to always have been a piano in our house wherever we lived — everyone should have one.

When I was growing up, we had a Vose, a small and sweet grand piano. My piano technique expanded in my late teens. I needed a sturdier instrument, and my mother and I went to Jenkins Music Company in KC and I picked out a medium-size Steinway which my mother arranged to pay for little by little. My father, when he heard about this, although he approved of the piano, was not too pleased with the financial arrangement, and he paid for it outright. (It stayed with me until, years later, in Santa Barbara. I had a chance to buy a concert grand, a nine-footer that sits downstairs as I write.)

My mother was clairvoyant and kept track of us, I think, in her thoughts. There was the terrible Sunday in May, 1944 in church when she suddenly felt ocean waves crashing and pounding over her head — it was at the instant, we learned later, that her son, George, was losing his life in the waters of the South Pacific after the crash of his plane.

She loved to hear us make music, and her favorite pieces that I played on the piano were the big ones — "play me my Chopin ballade" — that took effort and strength to play.

Myrtle Casebolt Diemer (1915)

My parents retired to a house they had built on a lot in southeast Kansas City and my sister and her family had built next door. My father died soon after retirement. He had bought two small farms near Centerview and cattle was raised on one of them, and money from the intermittent sale of cattle sustained my mother during the five years that she outlived my father.

When we think that we children are the important beings in our mother's life, we find that the light in her eyes is not the same when her beloved husband, our father, dies.

I can think of no other blessing than to have had a mother to love in life, and after death even more.

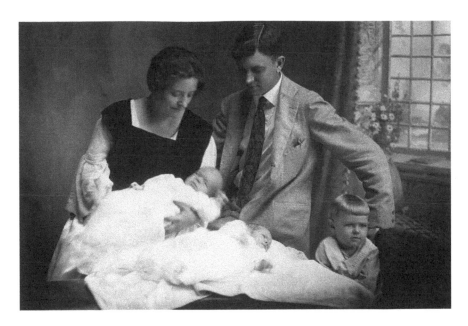

(Top) Mother and Father at the birth of my twin brothers George and John in 1920. Sister Dorothy is in the lower right; (Below) The family gathered at Selmo Park in 1952. Mother and Father are top left with sister Dorothy's family next, including husband Wick, baby Alan, Betty (l) and Terri (r). Then Grandmother Lizzie Casebolt and Emma Lou. John's wife Lois, far right, holding René with George III.

George Willis Diemer. 1937

My Father
George Willis Diemer

About one's father. (The beginning is human interest, the rest is biography, and brief-attention-span folks will perhaps not read that far.)

George Willis Diemer, my father, could read music and had a good bass voice. My sister found a Diemer ancestor in Louis Diémer, a 19th century French composer/pianist of some renown. Every family should have a genealogist. Larry Augsburger, my nephew-in-law; my niece René Krey; another niece, Terri Sims; my sister, Dorothy, have delved into family background — it's how history is made.

A child has only a self-centered impression of a parent, little comprehension of what that adult has experienced and is experiencing, knowing only the surface and how it relates to them.

My most-remembered times were the trips that we took as a family. Except for the trips to Colorado — to Boulder, where my father taught in the summers — they were trips to conferences in beautiful parts of the country and were the times when he was most relaxed, away from administering to a sometimes difficult faculty and the intricacies of presiding over a growing college.

And we stopped at almost every school building in those little towns we drove through, school buildings where education had been or was taking place.

I remember us stopping, on our 600-plus-mile summer trips from KC to Boulder, at the half-way town: Goodland, Kansas. It was invariably a hot day and my mother would

Two images of my father from the same approximate time of 1915, both reflecting a strong composure and dedication for the times.

have packed us a lunch to eat in whatever schoolyard was available. Always a thermos of ice water and tin cups to go around. "In those days" there were no fast-food places. Also no motels. No air conditioning in the car. But it was memorable, our family of seven together, anticipating eagerly the first glimpse of the Rocky Mountains. "There they are!" and "I saw them first!"

Those trips, and the evenings, when my father took me along while he worked in his office at the college and I could play on the pipe organ in the auditorium, were special to me.

When we had guests, he had them listening to his every word about important topics, or funny stories, occasional jokes, that we never tired of hearing. He had a habit, an art, of beginning a sentence and then taking a bite of food so no one could interrupt him (or want to).

He worked up to the day of his retirement and died soon after from cancer at the age of 70, having rarely visited a doctor before his illness or had more than a day or two away from work.

Now, in 2020, is a time of plague and pestilence, and the closing of schools and libraries is playing havoc with the education of people young and old. School systems, teachers, administrators are doing everything they can to keep their students learning and their minds active.

In my father's day there were no computers to aid in this endeavor. His fondest hope and the goal of his life was for people to be educated. He took his message to local, state, national, and international venues during his life.

As a child, he went to a one-room school in Missouri and while still a boy did some teaching in that school before going away to college at the urging of people around him — his mother, leaders in the community — those who were aware of his fine mind and who encouraged him to think of a future beyond his life in rural Missouri.

I think his first love was teaching, but because of gifts of organization, his general and broad knowledge, and an innate aura of authority as well as personal and physical

PRESIDENT GEORGE W. DIEMER

The above photo is of George Willis Diemer during his tenure as president of the Kansas City Teachers College prior to his becoming president of Central Missouri State College.

attractiveness — all those qualities led him on a career path from teacher to superintendent of schools (Excelsior Springs, Missouri), school principal and college president in Kansas City (Kansas City Teacher's College) and finally to a similar position at the college in Warrensburg (Central Missouri State College from 1937-1956, now the University of Central Missouri).

But his life work went beyond those positions. He generally became president of whatever national educational organization he belonged to.

Probably his most important appointment, from the US Department of State, was his selection as one of the American educators who went to Japan after World War II to consult and advise on the educational system in that country. (Thirty educators were invited by General MacArthur for that purpose.) He was similarly a consultant on education in Germany and elsewhere.

I think an educator should be educated. GWD was a student of history and science and read extensively — poetry even. Our father wanted all of us to be teachers. Not a bad ambition.

Going for a ride on the old Tin Lizzie in 1927 were Myrtle, George, John, George and Dorothy

Diemer Hall at the University of Central Missouri was named after my father. This image of the building is from the 1940s while he was there.

Emma Lou with her maternal grandmother, Lizzie Casebolt, on the steps of Selmo Park

Grandmothers

My grandmothers. I should say "our grandmothers", they having that role in the life of my siblings too, of course.

My father's mother lived in Brookfield, Missouri, and we visited her occasionally over the years. She had a modest house and one of her sons and his wife lived with her. She raised vegetables, and chickens. I have no idea how her family made a living, although Social Security must have helped out many a household after 1935. And my father sent money to her through the years. Whenever we left after a visit, she would give us one of her hens to take home for my mother to pluck and cook for our dinner. (My mother was not too fond of the first part.)

Amelia Diemer was a smart, sharp lady and probably mostly responsible for my father breaking ranks, going to college, and becoming a school administrator. I did not see Amelia very often, but I remember her as a kind (aren't grandmothers always kind?) woman who read the newspapers, kept up with the world, and was proud of her son and his family. She lived to be 91.

So did my maternal grandmother, Lizzie Casebolt. Lizzie Elnora Murphy Casebolt came to live with us when I was born, so she was part of the family for many years until her death in 1958.

My mother asked her to come and help her — with four children and the busy, full life in Kansas City where our father was president of the Kansas City Teacher's College (a school no longer in existence).

Amelia Diemer c 1944 (Far right- Others Unknown, including little girl who is not Emma Lou Diemer)

My mother was active in civic and church and school affairs and grateful for the abilities of my grandmother. We were grateful for her sweet and wise and spiky presence, and for her terrific cooking. And I remember as a child sitting on her lap and hearing her read Uncle Wiggily from the newspaper and Stevenson's *A Child's Garden of Verses*.

There was mutual respect and love between my father and Lizzie Casebolt. (He rarely called her other than "Mrs. Casebolt"; only in a rare moment of lightness and playfulness was she "Lizzie".)

She grew up in a small town in Missouri, DeWitt; her parents were lost to small pox when she was seven and she was adopted by a Judge Taylor and his wife. She married a fairly well-off man and had two children, my mother and my uncle.

However, her husband (my grandfather, John Henry Casebolt, whom I never met) was prone to unwise speculation — mines, I believe — and it fell to Lizzie to earn the living. And she did, by running a store and a small hotel, and saved the money as most Scots-Irish people do.

My grandfather was not careful with finances and finally my mother persuaded Lizzie to leave him and divorce him, a rather unusual occurrence in the early 1900s.

My grandmother and mother moved to Warrensburg and Lizzie bought some property and started "Casebolt Inn" near the college campus. She boarded students and served meals, with the help of my mother and one or two others, to as many as sixty young people every day.

As I said earlier, Lizzie came to live with us when I was born. I wonder sometimes at this loss of her freedom, her devotion to a daughter and family whom she loved, after a life really as a successful businesswoman. But how many little girls and boys are so lucky as to have their grandmother in their lives, reading to them when they are children, following their study years and careers, always there.

When we moved from Kansas City to Warrensburg, she chose the smallest room in the house, near a storage and game closet (where I used to hide out sometimes). She could look out at the yard with its spacious trees and the view of the long driveway. She must have spent many an evening watching us come home and waiting for us to stop by her room to say goodnight, which we always did.

Of course she read her Bible every night (I still have it). And she had many friends in our church (and the WCTU chapter in town). She lived the "faith, hope, and charity" ideal every day of her life. I remember listening to a conversation she was having one day with a friend who was being very critical of someone they both knew. My grandmother was absolutely silent. No ill words for anyone.

And did I mention that she played the piano — pieces she had learned as a young girl from an itinerant, German teacher who made a tour of the little towns in Missouri.

One becomes more wondering, (empathetic?) admiring when thinking about, trying to put oneself into the lives and existence of beloved relatives like one's grandmothers. We tend to think of loved ones in relation to ourselves rather than as individuals whose lives were probably far more important than our own.

Lizzie Casebolt with her husband, John Henry, in the 1890s. Emma Lou never met her grandfather.

Lizzie Casebolt's Inn (c 1915); George and Myrtle are in the photo on top row, far right.

Dorothy Hendry, baby Terri, Lizzie and Myrtle (c 1949)

Lizzie with great grandaughter Betty, daughter of Emma Lou's sister Dorothy and husband Wick (c 1948)

Emma Lou and sister Dorothy Diemer Hendry in 2003 in Huntsville

My Sister
Dorothy Diemer Hendry

These are very personal vignettes and you needn't read them, though they may ring a bell in your own life. How can, and should one, write about someone you've idolized for the entire time you've known them and after their death, too?

I will try to tell you a little about my sister, Dorothy. She was almost ten years older than I, and two years older than our twin brothers. It is hard not to love someone who loves you. Also, I am a sucker for people who are kind, and Dorothy and my family were 100% kind. Scrappy, teasing, scolding sometimes, but kind.

Of course she was loved by her husband and children and grandchildren and great-grandchildren. I lose track of generations and relationships at that point what with expanding extended families. (A new baby came into the world and I believe she is my "great-grand niece" since her mother is my great-niece and her grandfather is my nephew, son of my brother John. Whatever relation she is, her name, Aria Rose, is a musical one, and I hope she will be a musician among other things; her mother is a veterinarian, her father a teacher of school music, a composer).

But back to my sister. Dorothy hated war, especially the wars that were going on during the last years of her life, before her death in 2006. Strangely enough, her vehement anger toward the "war lords" may have helped to extend her life. And because she hated conflict, she was the most peaceful person I knew. She thought before she spoke, and even when she disagreed. She used only reason and forethought and tried to keep the waters calm. I think it's called tact, and diplomacy.

She read newspapers and books with amazing concentration and could be counted on to know the facts behind and have an opinion on whatever story or news item being discussed (she was an English teacher and a writer, for heaven's sake!). She was a fast reader, and I can remember as a child watching her eyes move quickly from line to line. Being a jumping and inefficient reader now who tends to stop often and think about a word or idea (or listen to a tune in my head), I admire readers who are not only fast but remember what they have read.

Before her marriage to an Army Captain, who eventually became a Colonel, an engineer, Dorothy was a flight attendant ("air hostess" they were called in World War II) and then chief hostess for her airline.

After her marriage she was a teacher/department head/consultant, and continued to use her talent as a writer and poet. She bore five children, four of whom survived to adulthood.

Dorothy could be dignified, occasionally stern. But I remember being convulsed with laughter as a child when she entertained me by making funny faces, making up funny stories. Children are great audiences for clowning adults.

However, she was a big sister by trying to get ten-year-old me to say something when we had company at dinnertime, and I rarely said anything, preferring to hear my father or my mother or a guest talk. And Dorothy would persuade me (a child, stubborn, shy?) to come downstairs and play for guests, even dragging me (gently) sometimes.

In her last months she would tell us in the morning of the dreams she had or the plots of audio books she had listened to during the night.

Mostly I remember that when I was with her, I felt I was worth something, and good, and she inspired me to be better.

Dorothy c. 1942 as an airline hostess with TWA

Dorothy and Wick with baby Terri and sister Betty at church during a visit to Warrensburg c 1949

Dorothy and Betty as a toddler c. 1945

Dorothy's Engagement Photo c. 1943

(Top) Wick and Dorothy's marriage in 1944 attended with Maid of Honor Janet Wood and Best Man Joe Smith; (Right) Dorothy and Wick during a happy moment at their home in Huntsville in 2002

The J.C. Nichols Orchestra (Kansas City school year 1930-31) which won the Southside Orchestra Contest; brother George with his trumpet is to the left of Dorothy with her flute on second from top row near the right hand columns, brother John is on front row right with his cello.

A family photo from 1938 (Left to Right) John, Dorothy, Emma Lou, George, Myrtle, and George

Dorothy Diemer Hendry   1918 - 2006

Her Life Was A Garden.

Her Fruit is Still With Us.

Dorothy at home, in one of
her rose gardens.

Dorothy—Last Years

A lot of music was written during the 1990s, and I'll write about it (mostly for my own record and you need not read); but if anyone is at all interested, first I'll relate something of the early 2000s. And Dorothy.

My sister Dorothy and my brother-in-law Wick — all of us really — were happy to realize that as the 1999 New Year calendar used up its pages, we were greeting a new millennium and still here — we all rejoiced. 2000! We had now lived in two centuries and were able to continue to experience the lovely things of life and to downplay a bit the things that were not so lovely.

For many decades I had traveled to Huntsville, Alabama, at least once a year, sometimes twice, to visit my sister Dorothy and brother-in-law Wick and family: Betty/Larry, Terri/Richard, Bonny/Steve, Alan, and eventually the grandchildren of Dorothy and Wick. At each visit, whether in the summer or the winter, some of them met me at the airport and soon we were in Sunset Cove, in the southeast part of the city, and entering from the garage the familiar kitchen and family room of the Hendry home.

If it was in summer, there would be roses on the table and in "my" room, and the latest books, and the sweet, kind, keen presence of my sister and the spicier persona of my brother-in-law. In the earlier days their children, when they were small, would gather around me expecting to hear exciting tales of the West (which were not forthcoming, and the kiddies soon drifted away — but the love was still there). I was not the most entertaining Aunt, except at the piano.

In the summers of those first years of the century the rose garden was the most spectacular it had ever been, with I think at least 400 rose bushes that my sister had planted and tended, reaching their peak of blooming. She shared numerous pails of roses with friends all over town and even brought some with her on one of her trips to Santa Barbara — encased in ice and ready to unfold.

I think that during some years when there were difficulties she needed to solve, she donned her garden gloves and took her cart out to the gardens and enjoyed while she worked the quiet and the fragrance of rose varieties that she could name, every one.

Over the years, the gardening went along with teaching and writing and cooking and reading, being with so many friends and church and travel with Wick and as the mother-always-there for their children — it was a busy, happy and full life.

In 2003, in January, I made my trip to Huntsville and Dorothy, as usual, had plans for us: one day we visited a garden center to look for new plants and bought some of those tiny cloth birds that you clip onto Christmas trees or drapes; another day we shopped at the farmers' market for food items; we went to the meeting of her book club in the home of one of her dear friends; we sat in on the poetry group meeting at a favorite small bookstore and Dorothy read one of her poems and listened to the others. And we gathered together as a family.

One day we went to see her doctor, a gracious and empathetic woman to whom Dorothy had gone before and who at this time was relating the results of a recent blood test.

When we returned home, Dorothy went to her computer and looked up words her doctor had written down. Multiple myeloma. Dorothy read the definition, the description, and I remember her voice to this day saying "Oh, dear."

I will not dwell on the aspects of this condition other than to say it is often — at that time usually — fatal, and Dorothy, over the next three years went weekly to the cancer center at the hospital for treatment, trials of new medicines. I visited more frequently during those years and went with Wick to wait during the two hours or so Dorothy was receiving some new drug, some new "cure".

Betty Hendry Augsburger arranges the candles on Dorothy's birthday in 2004; John and Sam Sims (grandsons) above Wick and Dorothy

You would have to know Dorothy to know that she made those visits almost festive, bringing along her portfolio of magazines for us to read and being always, always cheerful and hopeful and beautiful. There was never a time that she was not beautiful, her soft hair remaining intact and abundant.

I had thought that my sister would live to be 100, at least. She was the healthiest of us. She had birthed five children. She had gone through other adjustments of the

Dorothy's book on the life of her (and Emma's) grandmother Lizzie Casebolt entitled *Looking for Jency*

body that older people go through — get through if they are strong and determined.

Every bit of music I wrote during that period, thinking of the sister I had idolized all my life, reflected the despair and sadness I felt.

I thought of it now during the almost-confinement we as a nation, a world, are subjecting ourselves to, to suppress the spread of the virus that has taken more lives in the United States than any other country.

Dorothy was advised to stay at home, to try to let the treatments keep her living, and she did. She said once that it was a warm and almost contented time, her husband there, always, every night, every day. And her three daughters who lived not far away. There were still books and games, and meal-planning at night when sleep escaped her.

And Dorothy was writing her book about our grandmother, Jencey, which we published later, and she was collecting her poetry, several hundred poems to which she wrote prefaces and had us help her print and have bound. I think she knew that her poetry was one of the gifts she would leave behind.

And her dearest love, Wick, took care of her and lived barely a year after her death in 2006.

I have known exceptional, valuable, loving, wise, kind, strong, creative people. Dorothy was one.

Dorothy and Wick smile during an adventure overseas in the 1990s

Dorothy and Emma Lou enjoying the beach on a visit from Dorothy to Santa Barbara in the 1980s

(Top) Grandson Scott and wife Marianne Pfitzer attend to Dorothy in her last week of life; (Bottom) The family, coming from all across the United States, attended Dorothy's funeral on March 25, 2006 and pose below at Wick and Dorothy's lily pond in Huntsville

Dorothy and Her Poetry

This is about someone I knew very well.
She was there when I was born.
I was there not long before she died.
She was a poet all her life, but also:
A flutist
An English teacher
A flight attendant and later a trainer of flight attendants
A climber of mountains
A scout counselor
A life saver
A good swimmer
Lover of Earth
Hater of war and destruction
Expert gardener
Rosarian
The wife of a colonel and engineer
The mother of five children
Four are still living
Eight grandchildren
Nine great grandchildren
Many nieces and nephews
Two brothers

A sister.
Here is a poem she wrote in her teens:
"Joy and Sorrow"
> *Pain and ecstasy are never separate.*
> *The eye burns with the beauty of*
> > *sunlight on dancing water.*
> *The ear is painfully attuned to*
> > *a crying violin.*
> *The heart aches with the glory of*
> > *human love.*
> *Joy has strangely some core of sorrow,*
> *And a bitter day starts the flow of*
> > *wistful memories.*

And one written not long before her death:
"Experiment"
Nowhere in the cosmos —
nowhere among the glowing
beakers of God's laboratory —
moves and breathes another body
like unto you, O Earth —
fragile, beauteous Mother
of all plants and creatures —
even of our fractious human selves.
Help us to understand you,
Mother Earth, and to respect
your other children.
Gentle our spirits lest
we so hurt and maim you
that God, before he heals
you, hurls our loveless

cinders into a black hole of
failed experiments.
And she had a fine and wicked sense of humor
and wrote limericks:
"Conversation"
Though stylishly senior and gray,
We never lack something to say.
  A topic remains
  With endless refrains:
"O where are we aching today?"
She wrote hundreds of poems
We will collect.

George (left) in his Marine formals and John (right) in 1943 before George left for service during WWII; George died in the Pacific in a plane crash during service

My Brothers
George and John Diemer

We could spend forever writing about our family, couldn't we? A book could be written about each and every member, most lives containing happiness and tragedy. And one's brief childhood is compressed — until we unfold its details and remember parts of it as our family comes into our memory.

My brothers were identical twins — there is no closer relationship. They did not have long lives. George was a World War II Marine fighter pilot and died at age 23. John was a school principal in the Kansas City area and died of lung cancer at 43.

They were very similar physically of course and had the same kind of sense of humor — sardonic, wry, boisterous sometimes, clowning even, delightful. George was the more serious and that side of him deepened in his early twenties when he "joined the service". He was a physics major along with music and taught school after graduation, and learned to fly, and was engaged to a wonderful young woman, Elinor Toole.

George liked for things to be perfect. He at one time, when he listened to me, a ten-year-old, practicing the piano, told my teacher, Mrs. Payton, that I was making too many mistakes. She relayed this to me gently and although I was a bit offended, I practiced more diligently and, I think, improved greatly.

George did not like conflict, argument., saying "life is too short".

On his last night at home, after all his training as a
Marine fighter pilot and soon on his way to the war in the
South Pacific, he went into my mother's room to tell her
good night. After he left my mother said she reached up
and felt his tears on her hair.

John was, like our mother, a lover of people and quick
to laugh and be naturally affectionate and personable. He
majored not only in music but also Industrial Arts and he
built things, a small car, a desk, useful objects. He went
on to graduate school, majoring in voice, and eventually
put all his talents together and became first a teacher and
then a school principal who was knowledgeable in many
subjects and could sing to his pupils, which he did on
occasion. And he and Lois Wenger married and brought
four children into the world.

George and John had many talents — in music,
making things, working on older (but fancy) cars — in
which they could drive backward at quite a speed down
our long driveway.

I could hear John practicing on his cello in an upstairs
bedroom and stomping on the floor when he wasn't playing
something just right.

And George sometimes went into one of the closets
to practice his cornet when there was company downstairs.

And in college they had a dance band. Not a rock
band (rock hadn't been invented), but more of a "big band"
similar to Glenn Miller, Benny Goodman, etc. The band
didn't have guitars or synthesizers or an electronic piano;
it had saxophones, clarinets, brass, double bass, percussion,
acoustic piano. George was the leader, with his cornet;
John played double bass. The band practiced in our house,
in the music room, and I listened.

They took the band around areas in central Missouri
and played for dances and various celebrations and made
a little money for college expenses. They wrote many
arrangements of current popular music and perhaps some
pieces of their own.

Young boys George and John c 1932

In the early mornings I would hear one of my brothers, usually George, at the piano downstairs working on chord progressions and trying different positions and ranges. There was one progression of two chords that I remember very well. It was like a beautiful "Amen".

George and John in 1942

Emma Lou and John on horseback c 1941

John Irving Diemer

George Willis Diemer II

Lois Wenger Diemer at the time of her engagement to John in 1943

Lois Wenger Diemer

When you are writing an autobiographical work, which these stories are, you find that probably the most interesting parts have to do with people. Being human, we seek out creatures like ourselves. In a crowd our eyes fall upon persons of our own age. I think babies notice other babies. Old people notice other old people. Well, you get the idea.

I've written about colleagues, but mostly in relation to our mutual musical interests. When writing about family, one's feelings and remembrances become more personal. I've written about my immediate family that I knew well — my grandmothers, parents, sister, brothers; but not, if at all, about cherished in-laws and the children of my siblings. I wrote about my brother-in-law, Wick Hendry, because I saw him the most, at the Hendry home, wherever he and my sister, Dorothy, lived.

But I must tell a little about my brother John's wife. She was Lois Wenger, one of John's students when he taught music in the Washington, Illinois schools. She was no doubt the brightest of his students and became his assistant in the music program. And they fell in love — he 24, she 17 (a year older than me).

Lois was a vivacious, mature young woman and probably a little dazzled by her attractive young teacher. When John's twin brother, George, lost his life — following the crash in a fighter plane, a Corsair, in the South Pacific in World War II in May of 1944 — John lost probably the love of his life. Lois filled a great need for him and she and John were married in July of that year.

Through the years of career-building and trial occupations Lois was his partner and bore him four children: George Diemer III, René (Krey), Jack (John II), and Dee Dee (Deidre). Lois excelled in a dress designing/making business in their home, and was helped in this endeavor by a longtime family friend, Dick Davidson.

Lois sang alto in the choir that John conducted in their church. She helped him in a furniture-refinishing business that he had for about a year (until the fumes from the materials became detrimental to them both). John entered the education field, ultimately becoming a school principal before his death from lung cancer in 1964 at the age of 43.

Lois was left with their four children, the youngest (Dee Dee) six years old. I will leave it to others to write about these remarkable offspring of Lois and John, just as I leave it to others to write about the equally remarkable four children of Dorothy and Wick. A book could be written about each of them.

But Lois — I remember her beautiful hair and quick awareness and intelligence and her loving spirit. Soon after she and John were married they took a trip to Colorado with my parents and me. Two cars, keeping track of each other for all the miles. John and Lois very affectionate together, young and in love.

We had gone to their wedding in Washington, Illinois in July of 1944 and met Lois' parents, Erwin and Irene Margaret (Spring) Wenger. It was a warm day of course and I remember that the pianist started the recessional too soon and had to keep playing the opening notes (having played for many a wedding I know how she felt). John had adopted the Lutheranism of Lois' upbringing, a denomination carried on with force in the future generations.

And then there were all the years of child-raising for Lois and John and frequent visits to Warrensburg and then Kansas City. They made the long trips to Warrensburg by night to avoid traffic. And when my parents and

John and Lois with baby George III after WWII

grandmother and I moved back to Kansas City, John and Lois lived just over the state line in Overland Park, Kansas and came to see us with their children, who delighted in playing with their cousins, the Hendrys, living next door.

Lois was there for John during career changes and probably spare financial periods. And with him for his last months as he succumbed to lung cancer.

After John's death Lois phoned me almost every Sunday. Always upbeat and bright.

Lois did marry again, a longtime friend of John's and hers, Charles Opel. He was a kind and steady father to her children and a helpmate for Lois.

On her last visit to her father in Illinois, Lois went up to her room one evening after dinner to rest, and passed away in her sleep, from heart failure. She was sixty. A beautiful wife and mother and friend.

John and Lois after their marriage c. 1944

Lois with Dorothy and Emma Lou

John and Lois with Emma Lou and Dick Davidson

Captain Wickliffe Byron Hendry in uniform during World War II

Wickliffe Byron Hendry

Wick (Wickliffe Byron) Hendry was my sister Dorothy's husband and the father of their five children: Betty (Dorothy Elizabeth) Augsburger, Byron Wickliffe (who died at 8 months old), Theresa Sue Sims, Alan Wickliffe, Bonita Jean Pfitzer-Gierhart. And Wick and Dorothy had eight grandchildren and a number of great-grandchildren.

Wick was spicy, a bit quirky, a fine engineer, an Army Colonel. He grew up on his parents' (Ida and Roscoe) farm in Kentucky. He had three sisters. His children will have to write more about him, but I will write what I know.

He was dedicated to Dorothy, and their marriage lasted from Christmas Day, 1944, to her death in March, 2006.

Wick died in June, 2007, and many of the family gathered for a service under a big oak tree that he had planted from a seed years before, below the garden at their house in Huntsville, Alabama.

We all loved hearing his stories from his days as an Army ordnance officer for two years in Alaska during World War II and stories of his farm life.

He graduated from the University of Kentucky and after service in the Army he was a mechanical engineer for Westinghouse in Kansas City, Missouri, head of the engineering department at the University of Kansas City, and then engineer/developer for the missile/space program for NASA in Huntsville, Alabama.

He and Dorothy met on a flight on which she was a flight attendant (air hostess) for TWA. They only had

time for a coke and then he left on a flight for service
in Alaska. They corresponded for two years; and when he
returned, they were married in First Christian Church in
Warrensburg, Missouri where Dorothy's parents had been
married in 1915.

I played for Dorothy and Wick's wedding. It was on
a very snowy Christmas Day in 1944. The Best Man was
an "old, brief flame" of Dorothy's, Joe Smith, and the Maid
of Honor was one of Dorothy's best friends, Janet Wood.
Don Wilson (my longtime friend) played the trombone,
Elinor Toole (our brother George's fiancée) sang.

I remember that at the close of the reception at the
house and as Dorothy and Wick were departing on their
honeymoon my sister was the happiest I had ever seen her.
My mother was worried about the newly-weds driving on
the icy roads but Don assured her they would just "float
over the ice" in their happiness and be safe!

Dorothy had several proposals from young men in the
years before, but something about that Army Captain, that
tall Kentucky man with his charming accent and reddish
hair had put her on the marriage course, with Wick, for
the rest of her life.

Wick was an attractive contrast to Dorothy's calm,
patient personality. They swam together, played bridge,
went dancing, traveled often, led orderly and admirable
lives, and produced four children who combined the
strengths of both parents.

A fifth child, a beautiful baby named Byron lived
into his 8th month. He had an intestinal defect that was
corrected by surgery, but there was poor post-operative
care in the hospital. Dorothy was beside her baby when he
died.

Dorothy and Wick came to Warrensburg for the
services for and burial of their baby. It was the only time
I ever saw tears in the eyes of that stoic, controlled Army
Captain, proud father, Wick.

Wick became especially close to his grandson Scott
(Bonny's son), and Scott enjoyed his Grandfather's stories
as we all did.

(Top) Emma Lou's visit with the Hendrys at Christmas c 1967, (L to R - Dorothy, Terri, Wick, Emma, Alan, and Bonny)

(Below) Wick loving his "girls" Dorothy and Emma Lou

Dorothy and Wick c 1945 after their marriage

Wick with grandson Scott in 1981; Scott is an emergency room doctor in Huntsville, Alabama and was greatly influenced by his grandfather

Wick and Dorothy were active members of the Huntsville community and their church, First Methodist. Dorothy said that it was Wick who, after their marriage, urged their attendance at church on Sunday mornings.

Wick was president of the engineers' society in Huntsville and continued his service in the Army Reserves for several years after leaving active service.

For many years Wick drove the 500 miles to his mother's home on the farm in Kentucky, and continued to supervise the work on the farm after her death.

I think, know that he wanted Dorothy to go with him and live on the farm after they had retired from their service in government and in education, but she preferred life in Sunset Cove in Huntsville. They both compensated by Dorothy having an abundant and beautiful rose garden and a copious vegetable garden, and Wick periodically mowing their lot and the vacant lot next door and keeping the house and cars well-maintained.

In later years Wick helped his daughter, Bonny, purchase a 30-acre farm a few miles away in Brownsboro, a familiar and comforting place he could visit and sometimes work.

Wick attended with Dorothy the Rose Society meetings. He encouraged Dorothy's writing — her poetry and her book *Looking for Jencey* that she was writing at the time of her illness and death.

Wick was an intriguing, interesting man. When I was visiting and played the piano, he would sit in the adjoining study or come into the living room to listen.

Another fact. He spent, after retirement, many diligent hours at his desk reading scientific journals and managing the investments he and Dorothy held, and was able to leave his children some financial legacy. Most of all, they had a fine, occasionally unpredictable, but always strong and dependable man for a beloved father.

He was the love of Dorothy's life and she of his....

(Top) Emma Lou and Wick enjoy riding the horses at niece Bonny's farm near Huntsville

(Top) Emma Lou and Wick exhausted at the airport while awaiting flights; Dorothy took the picture

Lois, Emma Lou, George and Myrtle with the grandkids, George III, Jack, René at Selmo Park in 1956

John joins his family

Another Family

I have "another family". There are many families of course — families tend to grow. But I wrote a bit about the Hendrys, my sister Dorothy and brother-in-law Wick and family, and now my brother John and sister-in-law Lois, and their children: George III, René, Jack (John, jr.), and Dee Dee (Deidre).

I'm not writing about each member, each close relative of mine — maybe later, or waiting for them to do that. Each person is unique, different, one-of-a-kind and other clichés you can think of.

But my brother John was not so unique: he had an identical twin, George, and if George had not chosen to be a fighter pilot, he, too, would have brought forth a family with his fiancée, Elinor Toole. But it was not to be.

My mother and father and grandmother and I moved back to Kansas City (Missouri) when my father retired from the college in Warrensburg, and he died soon after.

Every fourth of July we drove the 14 or so miles from southeast Kansas City to Overland Park, Kansas where the "John and Lois Diemers" lived. My mother would put out our big flag early in the morning. (Incidentally, that flag is a symbol of our country and not of a political party or person — one must make that clear...).

As we drove, my mother would count the flags we passed that people had displayed outside their homes, and there were quite a few.

At John and Lois' house the two families would gather and have the usual fare broiled outside on a grill (by John) and fireworks afterward in the lot, the "back 40" where we also played at baseball on some visits.

After all the activities — food consumption and fireworks — we assembled inside in the living room. Have you been, ever, in a room full of your close, mostly blood, relatives and been aware of the phenomenon of actually sharing so many traits and resemblances? Sometimes, in the few, larger reunions of our extended families it was necessary to try to become acquainted with all those persons. Have you had that experience?

Also, on those holiday get-togethers there was some music, but mostly talking among the adults. And the children playing.

John and Lois brought their children to our house sometimes, and all the children (you'll remember the Hendrys lived next door) played games on the driveway between the houses. There was a rather large doghouse my mother had gotten for our dog, Jolie, and the children took turns climbing up and jumping off. (It doesn't take very young humans long to find fun things to do.)

And all those children, eight of them, were so happy to be together. I cannot remember any fights or angry words.

I remember, however, the visit I made to Overland Park, flying from Arlington, to be with that family when John died. The four children, the youngest six years old and the others barely into their teens, sequestered themselves in a room upstairs that day, I think reenforcing their filial unity, before greeting those who had come bearing sympathy. And of course that bond is still in force.

There was naturally a lot of humor and laughing in the various gatherings — John was a great entertainer of children — remember that he was a popular school principal. And Lois must have appreciated his lack of ponderousness more than anyone.

We who have no children of our own owe much gratitude to siblings who share their sons and daughters with us.

John, Emma Lou, Lois, Myrtle and George c 1947

Marilyn in front of my Steinway

Marilyn MacKenzie Skiöld

There are stones, pebbles, grains of sand, that have among them a few that shine, glisten, catch your eye more than the rest. And stars in the sky, so distant but so brilliant, changing, almost disappearing. There are people like that. You want to take their hand, show them to your friends, write about them, get to know them.

Marilyn is like that. She is ninety years old (in 2021). A friend calls her "Mariposa" — butterfly. Because she is quick, colorful, sometimes hard to hold onto. She is active, agile, moves easily, likes to take walks and wishes there were a pool handy so she could swim. The ocean is near, but maybe a bit cold, better for women younger than 90?

I knew about Marilyn before I met her. My friend, Phyllis King, went to school with her, worked with her in the same library in Minneapolis, spoke to me about her. But I didn't meet Marilyn for some years until a trip to Sweden where I did get to know her daughters — Mari and Ann and Lisa, Marilyn's then-husband, and many of her friends there. Her Swedish family was/is invariably tall, and handsome. Marilyn is like a bright jewel among them.

She left Minnesota to marry that handsome man, Olof Skiöld. She had graduated from the university and begun to teach when she met him, and it was an instant attraction, and after their marriage he whisked her off to Malmö and twenty-five years of living in the country that became her second home. I can imagine, can hear her mother calling

"Marilyn! Marilyn!" as she watched her daughter depart on the plane to New York and a ship that would take her to a country far away.

Marilyn and Emma Lou at home (c 1990s)

And Marilyn, with her quick lingual ability, soon learned fluent Swedish and continued teaching and birthed three beautiful daughters — Mari and Ann and Lisa — and made many friends, both Swedish and English, and presided over the various homes she and Olof lived in, the last being the spacious Asklunda in southern Sweden, Skåne.

Both her parents went to Sweden for visits. Her father, John Kenneth MacKenzie, is someone Marilyn talks about with much love and admiration. His father, Donald, was a Methodist minister, down from Canada, and died from a heart attack in Duluth after a WCTU conference, and left his wife, Grace Celeste Blood MacKenzie, with three young children, of which John Kenneth was one.

John Kenneth graduated from university, worked for a time for a hardware company and then for Prudential Insurance, where he eventually became an area manager. John Kenneth was an avid reader, and his daughter, Marilyn, keeps several books going at once, some in English, some in Swedish.

Marilyn's three daughter (c 1980s/L to R) Mari, Lisa, and Ann

Marilyn's mother, Leah Trefethen McLean, worked for the newspaper, the *Minneapolis Star Tribune*, for some years. Leah's mother was Mary Elise Murch who married Wesley McLean. Leah's grandmother — Marilyn's great-grandmother — was Nettie Sloane Murch, whose father served in Congress, was Secretary of State of Ohio, and Treasurer of the United States from 1850-1853.

I always felt/knew that Marilyn has an illustrious background, as did her husband, Olof, whose mother was a Baroness (Funck) and whose grandfather was a millionaire in Sweden (who lost his fortune and then regained some of it). Some of his inheritance passed on to Olof, and with it Olof and Marilyn were able to build their first house in Sweden after their marriage.

Olof Skiöld in Sweden in the 1980s

Back to Leah, Marilyn's mother. Leah's brother, Kent Edgar McLean, was a favorite of Marilyn. Uncle Kent had wanted to be a doctor, but he worked for a magazine company and was killed in his early fifties in a car crash caused by a drunken driver. Another favorite relative of Marilyn was her great aunt, Margaret (Aunt Mockie).

Marilyn has no brothers, but is very close to her sister, Sharon, who is four years younger. As of this writing, Sharon phones Marilyn from Florida, every day.

I find the racial mix in Sharon's family very interesting. Her older daughter's first marriage was to a Black man and she had two children (and later married an Englishman), Sharon's son married a stunning black woman, and her other daughter married a man of Hawaiian descent.

Marilyn c 1980s

I know Marilyn's family almost better than my own (which is quite a bit larger and equally fascinating), and her three daughters and other family members have made frequent trips here. Their almost-annual reunions in exotic places in the world are endlessly fun to hear about. Indeed, I've spent many an hour listening to Marilyn talk of her family and travels, of amusing incidents, observations. It is sad that for the time being those travels have been curtailed because of the COVID-19 virus.

Marilyn is one of those people who is endlessly interested in other people, and soon establishes a close rapport with them. She has friends (and family) who delight in her listening ability. She is alert and quick to respond and socially adept and involved.

Her daughters need to write about their mother, certainly the most interesting woman they will have known, particularly from the standpoint of her dual life as an American and her life as a wife and mother in Sweden. It was not easy for her to return to America after many years in Sweden. She made a life here in Santa Barbara, always working (the *News-Press*, the Museum of Art especially) and in later years becoming the care-taker of numerous dogs and a few cats, staying in clients' homes to care for the animals and sometimes bringing them home with her. I believe she has had 40 or 50 or more close clients who appreciated her care of their animals. On our walks Marilyn speaks to every four-legged being, without fail. And of course wins over every two-legged person with her smile.

Long live Marilyn Joan Elizabeth MacKenzie Skiöld!!!!!

Marilyn has always been playful and full of life. An outdoors person at heart, she is seen (top) on the beach and (bottom) at Yosemite on opening day with Emma Lou near a beautiful frozen lake.

Don Wilson, longtime friend and erstwhile companion of Emma Lou taken around 1946

Donald Elmo Wilson

Have you ever known someone who was so perfect, so pure, so kind, generous — all those good qualities — that they seem unreal in retrospect or even in present reality? My sister was pretty much that way. And a local friend, Carolyn Gell, seems like that to us. They are quite hard to criticize, their lives almost faultless. I say "almost" because there must be something about them that one can question. But why should we?

One day, long ago, in the summer, I think, when I was barely sixteen and had long hair and a young face, I was playing the pipe organ in Hendricks Hall at the college in Warrensburg. For some reason I looked around and saw, coming down the aisle rather excitedly, a radiant young man. He was in the garb of "summer whites", part of the wardrobe of Navy men. (There were, on campus, about 400 sailors of the V-12 unit that were enrolled/stationed there and who lived in Yeater Hall, next door to my family and me.)

In my memory he seemed to have a light behind him, an aura that with really vivid imagination you might describe as angelic. Or is it because over the years he has attained that stature in my mind?

He came down to the organ and said something — probably that he liked the music, the sound of the organ, my playing.

Some days later we found ourselves at a meeting of young people at my church — his, too, apparently. And I remember that when I laughed at something, he laughed, too, looking at me empathically. I believe it was after that meeting that he walked me home (in Warrensburg distances are not long, my house only a few blocks from the center of town).

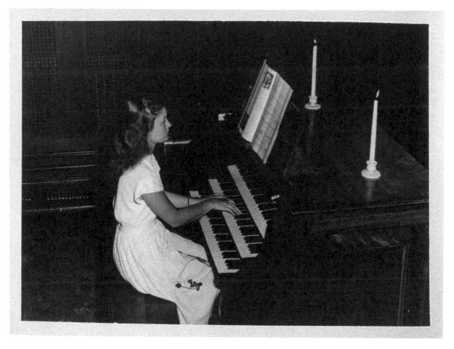

Emma Lou playing the organ at Hendricks Hall at Central Missouri State College as a teenager where she first met Don Wilson.

When we approached the house (Selmo Park, home of the college president), I think he was surprised. I don't think he knew I lived there.

Whether I was aware or not, it was the beginning of a long friendship. Don Wilson. He was a musician, a trombone player. He became so much a part of my family that his name appears naturally when I think about them. I believe it was assumed that I would marry him.

When he came to see us, I would greet him summarily at the door, maybe a little dismissive in the unfeeling manner only a teenager can express. Undeterred, he would go in search of my grandmother or mother, knowing that they would be delighted to see him and give him warm greetings in contrast to the coolness of that unsentimental young girl.

Don and I played game after game of checkers — I seemed to usually win, but in thinking about it wonder if he occasionally orchestrated that. We took bike rides around town, sometimes to the cemetery — like a park, quiet, lovely really, on the edge of town. We drove to Lake of the Ozarks and rented a rowboat and came back home sunburned and happy after a pleasant day.

Almost every Sunday he came to dinner at our house, walking the few yards from Yeater Hall.

After I graduated from high school I enrolled in music school and some time before I left for Eastman he must have talked with my mother about his wish to marry me. He told her he had been offered a good position in Kansas City and would be a stable, secure husband. When he and I talked about it one evening, I remember coming home and my mother meeting me with questioning eyes, wondering what my decision was.

I think that of all the boys, young men who are suitors to young girls (and I was no exception) my parents and grandmother actually would not have objected, in spite of my young age. They had that kind of love for Don.

He came to see me at Eastman, hitchhiked part of the way, still in the Navy. A classmate asked me if I loved Don and I said, yes, I thought so.

I returned to Warrensburg for my Sophomore year and he, having left the Navy, enrolled in the college also. We continued much as before. I think he had a few dates with other girls/women. One of them, a rather risqué young person told me she could never marry Don (as if he would have asked her?) — I think she meant he was too perfect, too pure?

After that year at home I again left for music school, this time Yale. Don had continued his studies in Warrensburg and received his degree that year.

Some time after those last few months Don gave up and departed for his careers. And they were impressive: he became first an ordained minister and then director of teacher education at the University of Southern California. He married a woman who lived next door. She had been divorced and I'm sure saw in Don what I saw: a beautiful and kind person to spend a life with. Don brought her once to meet my mother. Strangely enough, I felt a little abashed that he would marry anyone but me! Such are childish thoughts.

Years later I also moved to California and Don, living in Orange County, contacted me. We met for lunch a few times at a restaurant in the Channel Islands.

Don and Alva had two children. I never met Alva but remember that Don's license plate bore her name. That is a funny thing to remember, but comforting somehow.

Some years later, Alva died and Don let me know. One Easter Sunday he came to Santa Barbara and after dinner we took a walk down by the ocean. He told me that in those long-ago days he had wanted me to love him.

I learned from him, some time after his visit, that he had married again. And a few years later he died. At age 65, which in this day and age is incredibly young.

Would you believe that in those golden days in Warrensburg I only "allowed" him an occasional kiss on my cheek? Kissed by an angel, I guess.

Don joins the family on a weekend activity at Selmo Park c 1945
(Back row) Don, Emma Lou, Lizzie, George, Myrtle, Fayette and
Mabel Fisher; (Front row) Elinor Toole, Wick and baby Betty and
Helen Hamilton

Emma King and morning glories at Selmo Park, 1946

Emma King and Cemeteries

Many people find cemeteries scary, gloomy, places to stay out of. I, and probably many others, are fascinated by them. They are quiet for one thing. And when one stands at the tomb or the marker of a famous person or a relative, it is a chance to remember that person and what he or she did for the world. I can think of a lot of such resting places I've visited, among them Emily Dickinson's gravestone in Amherst, Massachusetts, Chopin's tomb in Pere Lachaise, Paris, Flannery O'Connors' in Milledgeville, Georgia, Eva Peron's in Buenos Aires, and the graves of the Kennedys in Arlington Cemetery where over 400,000 others are also buried.

The cemetery in Warrensburg, Missouri is named Sunset Hill. All my immediate family are there, so to speak: my grandmother, uncle, twin brothers, sister, father, mother. I guess I will "join" them one day. I like Woody Allen's quote: "I don't mind dying ... as long as I don't have to be there when it happens." But no one has ever gotten out of this life alive, someone else said.

My sister and her girl friends sometimes had parties near some mausoleum at Sunset Hill. My friend Don and I biked out there on occasion. I remember one summer evening when we sat on a hill and thought up as many adjectives as we could to describe the summer night. We decided "quiet" was the best one. Not very unusual, but accurate.

A good friend of our family who lived in an area of town that was near the cemetery was Emma King. She "worked for us", a cold expression to attach to someone who meant so much. Everyone works for someone, sometimes just for oneself. Emma King was part American Indian, part Black. She came to our house twice a week and kept it shining and clean. You'll remember that it was the residence of the president of the college, a state-owned house called Selmo Park, built soon after the Civil War. Downstairs it had a front living room, a music room, a large library, a spacious dining room, a breakfast room, kitchen, a sun room, and two "powder rooms". There was a front stairway near the front entry and a back stairway going up from the breakfast room; upstairs were five bedrooms, two baths, and a storage room. The basement had living quarters, laundry area, and a cistern that had been used in earlier times. And of course porches in front and back and even one upstairs that wound around two sides of the house. The garage was only big enough for one car — or carriage? — and there was a lily pool, a tennis court, and grape arbor/barbecue. In other words, it was a pretty neat abode and we loved it even though it didn't belong to us.

Emma King took care of the house and often helped out with receptions that took place there. She would come in the morning and work for awhile and then get the urge to sing while she worked, especially when I was playing the piano. I could hear her upstairs bursting into song during some piece that maybe inspired her to join in.

Emma King's husband, Perry, delivered our groceries, several times a week, and whistled, always cheerful. My mother phoned Davis Grocery nearly every morning. "What looks good today?" she would ask the man in the store. My grandmother, who did most of the cooking, clucked sometimes at the amount of food my mother had ordered. (You'll remember that my grandmother was part-Scots.) At that time we were a family of seven.

My mother was interested in and appreciated all religions, all people. She visited Emma King's church several times, quite different, especially musically I imagine, from ours. She tried to get Emma King to come to our church, but Emma always declined, saying "No ma'am! I'm a Baptist!"

Myrtle, holding baby Terri, while Emma King looks on, 1949

**The final resting place of George and Myrtle and George, Jr
at Sunset Hill Cemetery in Warrensburg**

Emma Lou and Dorothy at Bel Air Beach in Clearwater, Florida where the family enjoyed memorable times, 1962

The Sun and Families

Sitting on the deck this afternoon (taking a break from Finale — the music notation program that keeps you at the computer hour after hour), the sun was so bright I couldn't see to read. The California sun — oh, I know it's the same sun everyone has, but it's so different here — especially after a somewhat overcast morning. It's so brilliant it is almost unreal. And the air here, in the middle 60s, is typical: warm in the sun, cool in the shade. My mother would have loved it. I loved the sun in Missouri, too, orange and red in the sunsets behind our house in Warrensburg.

But it's the sun in Florida I want to talk about, and a family remembrance. In the 1960s, 1962 to be exact, I went with my sister Dorothy and brother-in-law Wick Hendry and their four children — Betty, Terri, Alan, Bonny — on a trip to Florida. My mother had died the previous year. I was living and working in Arlington, Virginia, and the Hendrys had moved to Huntsville in northern Alabama, beckoned by the space and missile program for Wick and for Dorothy the high school that would soon need a new English department head.

I had been present for their big move from Missouri, and so a vacation trip for all of us was in order. We were in two cars, and traveled all the way down Alabama to the Gulf Coast and then the coast of Florida, driving along the Keys to Key West. We had a glimpse of Ernest Hemingway's house and then drove back up to the mainland, through the Everglades to our motel in Clearwater and Bel Air beach.

It so happens that Marilyn's sister, some years ago, moved to Clearwater from Minnesota, and Marilyn and I visited her a few years ago and went out to the beach. The sand was so hot we couldn't walk barefoot, no way.

But back to the Hendrys. Our motel of course was right on the beach. We would all swim throughout the morning and the rest of the family would go in to enjoy the cool interior and I would loll around in the warm water. I'm not much of a swimmer. I just like to paddle around and then look for sea shells. (By the way, nothing bad happens in this story if there is something you'd rather do.)

One late afternoon we drove over to the tidewaters where the water is so clear you can see everything in the shallow depth, and we looked for crabs, brandishing our nets to scoop up the hapless creatures and took them back to the motel where Dorothy plopped them into boiling water, poor things. But delicious.

One evening we had all kinds of sea and land food — I had never tasted turtle before, a little spicy, also delicious. Poor turtle.

After Clearwater we stayed a bit in Pensacola, where my brother George once trained as a fighter pilot. The waves there were big and rolling, and we all had rafts to ride on. Except Dorothy and Wick, who swam out beyond the waves where the ocean was quiet and peaceful.

I spent many a happy time with that young family over the years. And most of them came to Santa Barbara for visits.

The sun in Florida is not so bright. There is a haziness, as though a rainstorm is coming, and a brief one usually does.

The California sun is miles away, and brilliant today.

The Trumpet Sounds Within My Soul

My brother George was a trumpet player; actually he changed to cornet by the time he reached college. You can look up the differences between the two instruments. He may have chosen the cornet because it could go higher, at least when he played it.

He and his twin brother, John, had a dance band in college and there was a rivalry between George and the leader of another band as to who could play the highest. George's fellow musicians were positive their leader, George, could. So they had George go to the physics lab and the professor tested the frequencies of the top of George's range. I have the article (thanks to historian Bruce Uhler) that writes about this, the scientific proof: George could hit the G above the G above high C. In other words, an octave and a 5th above high C.

When George went to the South Pacific as a Marine fighter pilot he took his cornet with him (which he named "Connie"). (We fervently wish he had joined the Marine Band instead.) In one of the Japanese bombing raids his cornet was reduced to a golden mass. George's fellow Marines found an old trumpet for him to play, to continue with one of his duties: playing "Taps" for fallen Marines.

My mother had bought a new cornet for him to play when he would return from the war, which was not to be. She gave it to a promising young musician at the college.

One doesn't forget the trumpet sound ringing through one's house.

I did not write any trumpet music or brass music until I was composer in the Arlington schools and wrote two different works: "Declamation" for brass and percussion (there is a recording on *YouTube* of the Marine Band playing this) and a band work, *Brass Menagerie*.

George hitting an octave and a 5th above high C on the cornet in a test with his college physics teacher

I remember sitting in the audience when "Declamation" was first played in one of the high schools and heard a girl student say when the drum rolls began "oh, I'm going to like this" (It makes a composer happy to hear positive comments).

The premiere of *Brass Menagerie*, whose movements describe different animals in a somewhat chamber music delicacy until the final movement, was accompanied by the rustlings and disquiet of the audience of high school students and during one movement a pipe bomb could be heard going off somewhere in the vicinity of the auditorium. However, the last movement is a full-band ragtimey, spirited piece and everyone listened. The work was published and was in the repertoire for awhile.

Soon after the Arlington residency I was organist at Reformation Lutheran in Washington, D.C., and one of the church members was Charles Erwin, who was first trumpet in the Marine Band. On special occasions he brought a quartet of band members to play in the service and I once wrote a florid arrangement of "A Mighty Fortress" for them. The "service" bands, as you may know, have some of the finest musicians in the music world.

I should add that there was/is more than one Marine Band, perhaps the main one being "The President's Own". The touring Marine Band, perhaps the main one, played once in Warrensburg when my family lived there, and my parents invited them all to tea. The conductor, William Santelmann, was with them. He was the 21st Leader/Director of the United States Marine Band, serving from 1940-1955. My mother was so proud to have the Marine Band in her house.

When I moved to California, the brass writing I did was a little more profuse. At First Presbyterian, where I was organist, a member, Philip Mann, was quite a good trumpet player. I wrote for him and our soprano, Audrey Sharpe, a setting from the book of Revelation of "And I Saw a New Heaven and a New Earth". It was with organ of course. We put Phil up in the balcony to play his part. (There were not seven trumpets; one was enough to ring out over the congregation.)

Another trumpeter in town was Ron Thompson. I not only wrote one piece for him, "Laudate" for trumpet and organ, but we recorded together an album *Music of the Baroque*. It was recorded at night at First Presbyterian to minimize traffic noise from State Street, and the recording company, Water Lily Acoustics, built a scaffolding for Ron to stand on above the choir loft, for the projection of his trumpet sound. It was a bit eerie, in the middle of the night, but memorable. That vinyl recording is something of a collector's item, and can be found.

On a stay in Fairbanks, Alaska, I met the players in the Borealis Brass Trio and later wrote two short pieces for them that they recorded. I had, a few years earlier, written a brass trio, commissioned, for another ensemble, and it was not too successful. It had several movements, and the trumpet player (it happened that all the players were women) complained about the lack of breathing space, places to breathe. She took a long time between movements to breathe. One of my friend Marilyn's daughters, Lisa, was with me in the audience, and wondered about the long pauses. I guess it takes more breath to play a brass instrument than a woodwind? I later transcribed that work for woodwinds.

And for Joan Dixon's writing-of-settings-of-the-psalms project I wrote works for trumpet and organ and bass trombone and organ. John Anthony was the trumpeter and Bryan Anton the trombonist. Later, Bryan asked me to write two works for eight trombones ("Palm Sunday" and "Chorale on 'Herzliebster Jesu'"), also published. That is the sort of request that is a delight to fill.

(At a concert at the Unitarian Society in Santa Barbara John Ernest, trumpeter par excellence, and I played the *Psalms for Trumpet and Organ*, and John performed the first movement while walking up the aisle. Choirs do that, why not instrumentalists — who've memorized their part?)

Another work written for Joan is a quartet for trumpet, horn, trombone, and piano, which can be heard on *YouTube*.

An unusual commission, from John Harbaugh, produced "Serenade for Flugelhorn and Piano". And another: "The Answered Question" for Amy Cherry, trumpet and Dan Cherry, trombone, and piano, on their album "Changing Times and Colors". In a live performance some of it is played offstage. (I'm not a prolific composer of theatrics, but try it on occasion.)

Lastly, one day a few years ago organist Alison Luedecke came through Santa Barbara and we had a visit downtown at one of the sidewalk cafes. She asked me to write a piece for her Millennia Consort, an ensemble of brass and percussion (and organ). Of course I said yes (never ask a composer to write something unless you really, really mean it) and I wrote "A Blast from the Past". I had heard her group at Stanford Memorial Church, a beautiful resonant space on the Stanford University campus. I sent the piece to her and it was played some time later at an American Guild of Organists (AGO) concert in San Diego. It is so revelatory to hear something you have almost forgotten you wrote.

Pipe organ and brass are a perfect fit — both are under wind power, both capable of a tremendous range of dynamics and great clarity. But all organists and brass players know that.

1 Corinthians 15:51-55 ESV

Behold! I tell you a mystery. We shall not all sleep, but we shall all be changed, in a moment, in the twinkling of an eye, at the last trumpet. For the trumpet will sound, and the dead will be raised imperishable, and we shall be changed.

SECTION TWO
Becoming a Composer and Teacher

The Disciples of Christ (Christian) Church in Warrensburg where Emma Lou played the organ as a teenager

Childhood
and Playing For Church

When I was a little girl, I was always taken to church and, when I was quite small, during the service I drew pictures or colored in a coloring book-anything to keep a young child busy, and the wise parent cams prepared to supply the child with diversions that would occupy her, especially during sermons. I can't remember crawling around under the pew or taking all the pencils out or whispering a lot. Maybe I did — we think of ourselves as perfect children (of God?) when probably we weren't. Were you?

But some of us, even when very young, do pay attention to the music. I like to think I did. When I was an innocent of maybe two or three, I saw a typewriter high up on a table in one of the church rooms and asked a kind lady if it played "Jesus Loves Me". So I must have been aware that machines sometimes made music. Like pipe organs.

I had played the piano since age 4 or so and began playing the organ at around 13. My mother wanted me to play the organ in church. It was what my grandmother did, in one of those small country churches in Missouri where there was a reed organ. I believe it was Miami, Missouri, where my mother was born. My grandmother of course not only played the organ for hymns but brought and arranged the flowers on the altar and prepared the Communion and straightened the pews after the service and added her cooking prowess to church suppers. Women have always made the church presentable and sometimes, I guess, be allowed to read the scripture or lead the singing. (And eventually actually be the Pastor.)

Church was a big part of my mother's and grandmother's lives and my father always taught bible class and served on the church board. In Missouri it was a foregone conclusion that one went to church. At the time I was growing up there were around sixteen churches in Warrensburg, population five thousand at that time. The churches, including the Catholic, all had "open" Communion except the Baptist church, which served Communion only to members. The Baptist church was across the street from the Christian Church (Disciples of Christ) where I eventually became organist.

Music? I can recall hearing Malotte's "The Lord's Prayer" sung innumerable times, especially once at the Baptist church when the tenor cracked horribly on the high note "for-*EV*-er". Funny what one remembers.

(And I can remember too many open-casket funerals, and the sad smell of flowers in the funeral parlor.)

At my church, the main service had the usual hymns of the time, and there was a more informal service earlier (good grief — we had "praise services" even then?) where the more boisterous hymns were sung gustily, like "Stand Up, Stand Up For Jesus" and "I Am Thine, O Lord" and "Brighten the Corner Where You Are", which I always thought of as "Bright In the Corner Where You Are". I played the piano sometimes for that service. And much, much later wrote settings of some of those hymns at the instigation of Dale Wood, who was editor at The Sacred Music Press. Those hymns had *Rhythm*!

My mother preferred more sedate, more theologically profound hymns like "The Church's One Foundation" and "Beautiful Savior". Our hymnbook didn't have the English beauties the Episcopalians sing.

Speaking of Episcopalians, before I started playing at my own church and before I played a pump organ for a few months at the Christian Science church (I was about 13) a nice lady in the Episcopal church asked me to substitute a few times there. I remember that I would sit at the organ and she worriedly placed piece after piece of music on the music rack for me to sight-read and play in the service. I dutifully played them, but recall that it was all a bit frantic.

(I've never had a desire to play in an Episcopal church, though I love the services, because of the volume of music one must play at the right time. Of course I have been confused sometimes in my non-liturgical Presbyterian service which is much simpler; one Sunday a few years ago I started the closing hymn with full organ before the Pastoral Prayer rather than afterward where it was supposed to be; the kindly associate minister, Judith Muller, hurried over and set me straight and I came to an embarrassed cadence. After the service when I was changing my shoes in the sacristy, the minister's wife, Kati Buehler, came in to greet me — I think to see if I was all right mentally; the stories that could be told about playing for church!)....

My first piano teacher, Mabel Payton, was a student of a student of this famed instructor, pianist and composer, Poland's Theodor Leschetizky

My First Piano Teacher
Mrs. Payton

Here is another little story, by popular demand (well, my niece Betty asked me). It is about music. And teachers. When I was a very young child, my mother and grandmother both played the piano and my siblings played their own instruments. As a toddler, I was fascinated from my vantage point on the floor at the way the piano keys went up and down and the sounds that came out.

Instead of banging on the keys, I began to pick out tiny melodies that I had heard and even make some up. My mother was well aware of this, and after teaching me a bit she enlisted a dear friend, Mabel Payton, to give me lessons. Mrs. Payton had studied in Europe with a concert pianist who had studied with a well-known pianist, who I believe was the Polish pianist/teacher Theodor Leschetizky and though she had not concertized, perhaps because of a rather frail constitution, she brought her own training to her pupils.

In my lessons she worked on hand position (having me hold a rubber ball, e.g., to encourage curved fingers — Horowitz's flat fingers not withstanding). But the music was the thing and *I refused to learn to read music.* Undaunted, the kind and gentle Mrs. Payton taught me by rote: Sinding's "Rustle of Spring", MacDowell's "Shadow Dance" and other fast-moving pieces that I loved. She tried to get me to read music. She brought various games for that purpose, to no avail. When I made up small pieces, she wrote them down for me. Just before we moved from Kansas City (Missourri) to the college town, Warrensburg, I was in a piano recital and my picture was in the paper, my curls and all (I was nine) and was quoted as saying I liked fast music the best.

In Warrensburg I was to study with the head piano teacher at the college. I went to my first lesson and she (Miss Schoen) put a piece of music on the rack and said play it. (I think visions of bratty child prodigy were dancing in her head). Well, I couldn't read music. I imagine she went "humph" and can remember her drawing up a stern, reproving look, maybe a "tsk, tsk". I went home humiliated, a little angry, and stopped playing altogether. No more music, no more piano.

Of course this distressed my mother. In desperation she phoned Mrs. Payton. To make a long story even longer, my mother arranged for Mrs. Payton to come on the bus from KC every two weeks and give me and my siblings lessons. I began playing again. Before too long I taught myself to sight-read, mostly from the necessity of accompanying my siblings on their instruments and eventually accompanying music students at the college. I went to the piano at every spare moment (there were no computers). Wrote music. etc.

Later I had other teachers — at the KC Conservatory, at Yale. All excellent. But Mabel Payton will never be forgotten.

Edna Billings and the Navy

Our local paper (*Santa Barbara News-Press*) has been getting smaller and smaller during this pandemic, and yesterday it was gone entirely (back today). Its size reminded me of the paper that was delivered to our house in Warrensburg every day. The paper person folded it into a neat little square and could easily toss it to our driveway (or bushes — which annoyed my father quite a lot).

At 14 I was organist at our church and studied organ with Edna Scotten Billings. Mrs. Billings came from Kansas City every week to teach organ at the college (now the University of Central Missouri). She was another good friend of my mother from the KC days and a wonderful, charismatic woman, a fine organist. She was choirmaster/organist at Grace and Holy Trinity Episcopal Cathedral in Kansas City. I believe at that time there were few women anywhere holding that important position in a major church.

Mrs. Billings, in the organ lessons, would tell her girl pupils to "play like a man" — in other words, play with assertion and conviction (rather than shyly and timidly as girls in that era were sometimes taught to be). I took her advice.

Our house in Warrensburg was back quite a way from the street and almost on the edge of town and when we moved there, there were wheat fields on two sides and far down one hill was the college stadium. Soon after we took up residence, a women's dormitory, Yeater Hall, was built on adjacent land, and during World War II the women were moved out and a Navy V-12 presence was moved in. So there were 400 sailors living next door to us.

In early mornings we could hear their drilling exercises and their calisthenics in the athletic field (that had been a wheat field previously) and at night we listened to the playing of Taps at curfew time.

My friend, Joan Turnbow, had a sailor friend, Byron Autry, who played the trumpet (and was the Taps player) and my sailor friend, Don Wilson, was a trombonist. They were both excellent musicians.

One evening the four of us were at my house and curfew came around. Byron didn't feel like playing so Don went out on our porch and pointed his trombone toward Yeater Hall and played Taps discreetly and beautifully. I imagine the young Navy men were surprised, hearing their goodnight song coming from the "big house" and on a trombone, but am sure it was relaxing.

The "big house" was torn down a few years ago. It was built about the time of the Civil War and was a Missouri state historical site but there was some deterioration over the years and the cost of renovation was deemed too much. I'll write about it at another time if anyone is still awake.

Navy midshipmen graduating before leaving for WWII in a ceremony on the grounds of Central Missouri State College

The sanctuary of Grace and Holy Trinity Episcopal Cathedral in Kansas City where Edna Billings was choirmaster and organist

"Go, Go, Mules!"— A pennant from the 1940s at what was then known as Central Missouri State College, now University of Central Missouri

Hendricks Hall at Central Missouri State College where Emma Lou played and performed

Teachers

"Suffer the little children". This particular "memoir" is about teachers. And children. One child. And there are no bloody episodes, no kidnappings, no beatings — so you may wish to turn to the news. If your preference is for tweets, this will not be of interest. Unless it rings a tiny bell....

I can remember very few teachers that I didn't like.

In Kansas City (Missouri) I went to the J.C. Nichols Elementary School, within walking distance from our house on Edgevale Road (where I was born). I walked to school and always looked back at my mother standing, waving in the door of our house, calling to me to be careful and "*Look Both Ways*" (for traffic).

Everyone loved the kindergarten teacher, Truth Spencer. She was kind and attractive and would come by each child's desk during the morning and I was always happy and proud when she stopped at my desk. Many years later she was a member of a church where I was organist and I think we both remembered those long-ago kindergarten days — I did.

My first grade teacher, Miss Pennington, was also sweet and kind and came to comfort me one day when I had an "accident" in front of the class and was crying. She also continued our knowledge of reading and writing.

In either third or fourth grade I did not get along with my teacher, whose name I can't recall (but will call "Mrs. W"), mostly because I was constantly bobbing up from my desk and being obnoxious, trying to see the clock. I can remember her telling me that because of my father's standing in the community I should be ashamed not to behave.

My mother became aware of the friction between Mrs. W and me and phoned her. By the way, my mother was at all times active in the local parent-teacher association, the PTA, usually president, and believed firmly in helping teachers, helping children. As an aside, she was instrumental (a pun) in raising money for musical instruments for J.C. Nichols school and we heard much about this, and later the instruments.

After my mother talked with my teacher she (Mrs. W) asked me to play the piano for the class, which I did on several occasions; and miraculously I began to like Mrs. W and she me. I no longer bobbed around at my desk.

We moved to Warrensburg when I was nine and I was in Delta Neville's fifth grade class. Miss Neville was head of the elementary division of the school. She was a genial woman, authoritative but not oppressive or mean (I think teachers can be mean sometimes for one reason or another).

The K-12 school was a training school for teachers from the college. Later, the name was changed to College Laboratory School and finally College High School. It was right on the college campus, in its own building, and students were able to attend programs in Hendricks Hall in the Administration Building some yards away.

Almost all the student teachers we had were excellent (my brother John was one, in music, one quarter, and it was fun having him as a teacher; we became good friends about that time — earlier, I think, I was a spoiled younger sister that he could tease).

In Miss Neville's fifth grade class one of the student teachers we had was a good looking and genial young man who spent the class time talking to us about sports or something away from the subject we were supposed to be learning; we liked him, but didn't learn very much.

My favorite teacher, in junior high school and perhaps all time, was Pearl Bradshaw. She was a kind of Eleanor Roosevelt woman, not beautiful, but wise and inspiring respect. She had us learn any manner of things like the names of the planets and how to write a check, and had us memorize poetry and recite it in class. Her military son was killed in the war not long after my brother George. Mrs. Bradshaw had no discipline problems. Her class of 25 or so pre-teens included a small, bright boy named Richard Emery (his father was on the college faculty); and when Mrs. Bradshaw would ask a question, Richard would always be the one to wildly wave his arms in the air and leap up from his desk to answer, usually correctly. Some of us girls may have had the right answer, too, but were too timid to voice it. (Those were the days when pupils had to raise their hands for any number of reasons.)

As high school progressed, we went forth from our home room to study art or language or science — or *Music*! Band practice was after school, and Mr. Losson was our amiable, talented conductor, and we met in Dockery building, a quaint old structure that alone survived the 1915 fire that devastated the campus. Old Dockery (which still exists) had a long metal tube, the fire escape, reaching from the highest floor to the ground and we as kids spent much time sliding down it.

But back to music: Magdalen Hendrix was our choral teacher and chose good music for the girls glee club, including a piece titled "Cherry Ripe". I've no idea who wrote it but I sang the second soprano part. Miss Hendrix also chose music to sing at assembly and the whole student body sang out of an imaginative song book that had a wide variety of music. One of my favorites was Cole Porter's "Night and Day". Try to imagine a bunch of high schoolers singing that. Miss Hendrix always became very nervous and irritable before we were to sing in a program. But she was a gem of a strict, well-trained musician.

There were a number of single women and a few married women on the college faculty. Some of those who were single had probably had relationships with men who were killed in the first world war. In my high school there were two English teachers that I especially remember: Ruth Fitzgerald, who also taught in the college and who directed our junior play, and Marion Conway, a dignified and learned woman who lived across from the campus in a small house with her mother. Miss Conway and I kept up a correspondence for awhile after I graduated from high school. I remember her neat, distinctive handwriting still. Why do we lose contact with those dear people who were our teachers?

My father, president of the college, was particularly supportive of women and respected their abilities as administrators and teachers. Pauline Humphreys comes to mind, a dean of the faculty at one time. And Monia Morris, who taught us algebra and later wrote a history of the college at my father's urging.

The motto of the college (now the University of Central Missouri) was "Education For Service". At least that was the inscription above one of the entrances to my old school, in those days. I may have been the only fifth grader to notice it.

A Freshman
at the Eastman School of Music

Music leads us on, does it not? If I had the talent to be a popular song writer and make lots of money, maybe I would have gone that way. But I wanted, I guess, to delve more deeply into the workings of music-making and figure out how to express in music those more complicated mental and emotional leanings that follow us through life.

My parents were in favor of my going off to music school after I graduated from high school. What could they say? So at seventeen I boarded a Missouri Pacific passenger train from Warrensburg (Missouri) to Kansas City and then New York City and ultimately Rochester. I was in some ways something of a baby. A very few years before, when I attended a two-week church camp, I cried for the first week I was so homesick. People were sympathetic and in the second week I was happy, playing the organ for the chapel services (it seems we kept singing "In Christ there is no east or west") and met a nice-looking boy who, back in KC, I introduced to my "godmother", Emma Serl, who lived at the Country Club Plaza in a beautiful residential hotel. But I soon lost touch with the boy of course in the bustle of teenage life.

Anyway, boarding the train bound for the East Coast I had a little stuffed lamb to accompany me, and I can remember talking on the trip to that lamb and telling it how sad I was to be away from my family. (The lamb said not a word.) I wonder how parents can send far away a daughter, in this case, and worry, worry, pray, etc. Of course sending a "child" away to music school is not quite like seeing a "child" go off to war.

I believe the trip to Rochester took about thirty hours. On later trips (to Rochester, and a couple of years later to New Haven) I traveled coach, but on this initial trip I had a "roomette".

Wayne Barlow, 2nd from left with fellow Eastman instructors, (L to R) Samuel Adler and Joseph Schwantner with Ted Price (music critic)

I arrived at Eastman that warm September day. All the women (girl) students were required to live in a dormitory. I have always hated dormitories, any kind of group living. I had a roommate who was a kleptomaniac. We both did some baby-sitting for a time at someone's house and one night I thought I was alone, except for the baby, and a son in the family came downstairs where I was innocently reading. To make a long story short, the family had been missing items from their house and knew either I or the other baby sitter was the culprit. She was caught on another night.

There were other instances of kleptomania, and I was happy to have a room of my own for the rest of the school year.

My mother came for a brief visit during the year and was a hit with the friends I had made. My parents always seemed able to travel to see their children wherever they were whenever possible. Bless them.

But back to music! I was in Wayne Barlow's theory class and I liked Professor Barlow — he reminded me a little of my brother George. He had us write down what he played — a 4-part chorale usually — and I enjoyed copying each voice and I remember the resonance of the piano and the sound of the chords. There is definitely a visceral reaction to music. Whoever said the overtone series is not with us all the time? Modestly speaking, I never received anything less than an A in theory. Or in composition.

My composition teacher was Edward Royce, a gentleman on the verge of retirement whose father had been a philosophy professor at Harvard, I believe. William Royce? I can find neither man on the web nor did I know any of Edward Royce's music. One memory I have is of him down on the floor trying to attach an electric cord, for what reason I can't remember.

He liked the compositions I wrote that were tonal and in a regular meter and pleasant; but when I came with a piece that was more dissonant, he was not pleased. However, I liked Professor Royce and can sympathize with his having to listen to all manner of music by young composers

One piano piece I wrote at that time was "Chromatic Fantasy" that had a rather contrapuntal beginning and a rhapsodic treatment of the theme and then a 5/4 variation with an *ostinato* bass. I played it in a student composer recital (in Kilbourn Hall) and I remember that Bernard Rogers, who was on the composition faculty, and with whom I would study some years later, liked the 5/4 section. It was a little "quirky", something composers come upon sometimes and should give in to more often. (to be continued)

Aerial view at night (top) and front (below) of the Rochester, New York Eastman School of Music

Going to Music School

"The unexamined life is not worth living."—Socrates. So that is an apologia for continuing these "memoir" stories. They may ring little or big bells of recognition in someone else's life. We tend to live day by day — well, how else can we live? — and pay not much heed to what has gone before and the reasons for why we are where we are in life (which, for all we know, could end at any time). So I'll continue writing about what I remember. I apologize for the "me"-ness and will try to mitigate that and write more about the people and circumstances that led/guided/sometimes hindered one person's path on Earth.

In a previous "memoir" I was in high school and pursuing music as my *raison d'etre*. I've had to reinforce that belief periodically because who of us can absolutely say we are of use to the world?

When I was sixteen my brother George lost his life — as a Marine fighter pilot in World War II. He was a budding composer, I think, and a fine musician. I could say that I continued what might have been his unfulfilled ambition, but that would be only half-true since we have our own trajectory that can't be denied.

I chose to go to a music school rather than a liberal arts college (though for my second year of study I did that, for reasons to be explained). After looking at the catalogs of several music schools I chose the Eastman School of Music, part of the University of Rochester. (I'll continue with this, but wonder if anyone is really interested, or should I keep it all to myself? — I can hear some yelling "keep it all to yourself!", but maybe someone else, some kind person, will encourage more "spilling of the beans", so to speak.)

Eastman as a Freshman and Howard Hanson

The director of Eastman at that time, and its first director, was Howard Hanson. He gave the welcoming speech in Kilbourn Hall and I never forgot it. Dr. Hanson was one of those composers (and conductor and theorist and pianist) who thought outside himself. I think he talked about humanity and the world and many branches of knowledge and goals in life. Whatever it was he said, I remember his mantle of dignity and kindness. During the year he invited every incoming student into his office for a brief chat, an occasion that I'm sure other students, like me, have remembered all their lives.

His music was/is full of unabashed expression, forbidden/looked-down-upon romanticism. Eastman was known musically, probably, as rather conservative and not avidly following the serialists and set theorists who were to come. Each music school seemed to be imbued with the style of its major composer — something I'll write about later, in another article. Eastman was known for its outstanding orchestral sound and for the Eastman Wind Ensemble and its conductor, Frederick Fennell.

At one of the concerts in Eastman Theatre Leonard Bernstein conducted, and I watched and listened from a balcony seat. He had, not long before, become famous as the last-minute, "fill in" conductor of a concert of the NY Philharmonic, and critics wrote that he liked to show off his profile while conducting. I admired him then, and now,

Howard Hanson, conducting in the 1930s

particularly his *Jeremiah Symphony* and *West Side Story* and other musicals, and his efforts as a peace maker.

Every morning — it seemed as though it were every morning — we Freshman would go up to a gymnasium in the building — an annex adjacent to the music building — and be given exercises, calisthenics. I kind of enjoyed that, but landed wrong too many times on the instep of one of

Kilbourn Hall at Eastman School of Music, where Emma Lou was welcomed as a freshman by Howard Hanson, is also a concert and recital venue.

my feet and limped around for a few days, accompanied by a fellow composer, Byron McCullough, who had a disability from childhood polio. "B.B." was a bass trombonist and later spent many years in a major orchestra, and we kept up a correspondence for some years. He was one of the few students I got to know, being absorbed in being a composer and not bothering with much socializing.

During that year, my friend Don Wilson came to visit. He was still in the Navy. I've written more about him in another story, if you are interested.

I studied piano with Blair Cosman, and he had me play everything detached, I guess in an attempt to improve my technique; I wasn't enamored with that approach, but have found it useful since, especially in organ playing which can be dreadfully, unceasingly *legato*. (His studio always smelled like antiseptic — funny what young people notice and remember.)

All of us were in chorus, and I remember that the conductor, whose name I have forgotten, spent what seemed like the entire hour on one chord, trying to create the perfect sound. It was interesting, but a bit exasperating. At that time I was not vitally "in to" choral music or writing it. At Eastman, it was the sound, the orchestral sound, that remained with me. There is nothing like a symphony orchestra, and writing for one, which I would do eventually....

Warrensburg
and Deciding on Yale

Being at Eastman as a Freshman composition major was something golden in my memory, and I would return there some years later, but at the college in Warrensburg, Missouri a Bachelor of Music degree had been added (I'll bet my father, president of the college, had something to do with that).

How does anyone ever leave a home that is filled with love and care? My sister Dorothy and my brother John had both married the year that our brother George lost his life in World War II, and the home life was my mother and father and my grandmother, who had lived with us from the year I was born.

My mother always made sure, too, that there was a family dog in our life since many children/young people (and beyond) need that presence, a being to share part of one's days. So we had gotten an English shepherd we named Jolie. When Jolie was a tiny young puppy and not feeling hearty my grandmother would hold her in the palm of her hand — and, I think, willed her to be well.

So not only the new music degree but my beloved family drew me away from Eastman for my second year of college. I believe I played organ again at my church and traveled by bus to Kansas City sometimes for piano lessons with Wiktor Labunski at the KC Conservatory and had a few composition lessons with Gardner Read, who was a visiting professor there.

At the college I was enrolled in a theory class taught by a tall, sympathetic woman who finally decided that my elaborate harmonizations of chorales and such really needed not much more traditional instruction and she pretty much excused me from the rest of the term. And

Celebrated pianist, composer and pedagogue Wiktor Labunski who taught piano to Emma Lou

my organ practice interfered with gym — hockey, as I remember — where I received my worst grade. And in the literature class we were assigned wonderful books, reports for which I resorted to the useful synopses in the *Digest* by Helen Keller (not the Helen Keller we know). I found that if I knew the gist of the novel and elaborated on it the teacher was more satisfied than with a laborious analysis.

My interest was in composing music, almost only that. I wrote to Eastman to see if I could be taken back, but admissions of service people, returning from the war, were taking up enrollment quotas. I researched various music departments and eliminated most of them, including Radcliffe (at that time an all-women college — why get a Radcliffe degree instead of a Harvard degree?). And I chose Yale, I believe because Paul Hindemith was there.

Paul Hindemith, the famous German composer and teacher, in 1923

Yale and Paul Hindemith

As I said before, I chose Yale because on the faculty was the esteemed composer, Paul Hindemith. I was also influenced by composer and teacher Edwin Gerschefski who studied at Yale and had stopped in Warrensburg on a lecture tour. Gerschefski came by our house and I played for him a set of descriptive piano preludes I had written and he recommended that I apply to the Yale School of Music to continue studying composition.

In my application I completed several harmonizations and other exercises that I was sent, and also had to supply some references. I was admitted.

As an aside, I wonder what my stylistic path would have been had I continued at Eastman in my undergraduate study. Yale and Eastman were quite different. Howard Hanson and Paul Hindemith—very different, but both terrific composers.

Women had been admitted to the professional schools at Yale for some years. When I entered the music school, there was one other woman composer: Violet Archer, a Canadian. She was in my composition class with Professor Richard Donovan, with whom I studied during my three years at Yale earning my Bachelor's and Master's degrees.

You will find it mindless and incredible that I didn't want to study with Hindemith, although Richard Donovan said I should. (I was the same rebel at Tanglewood a few years later when I chose not to study with Aaron Copland. There is no hope in us).

Reasons? Every composer at Yale wrote like Hindemith. Little Hindemiths. His style of counterpoint is addictive. I found his use of rhythm not very exciting. But the lines made sense and the putting together of the parts had direction and purpose and neat conclusions and no weak links. A linear dream! And it has influenced my style ever since. But I didn't want to study composition with him. (Yes, there is some shyness at work there, too.)

I was in Hindemith's two- and three-part counterpoint classes, using his text books; those exercises, which I liked immensely, were the foundation of his counterpoint.

In class he worked quickly at the blackboard adding line of music to line of music. He was a small man. He always seemed on the verge of being amused (I think geniuses are often amused). He knew everyone's name right away — he knew mine at almost first sight.

I remember an incident during a rehearsal Hindemith was conducting with the school orchestra. At one point he was exasperated with the playing and sat down on the podium with that amused expression on his face. He looked like a cherub.

What I admired about Hindemith most was his ability to write for any level of technical attainment and for just about any instrument and voice. This I have never forgotten. (More about life at Yale next....)

More About Studying at Yale

Universities. The one in Warrensburg, In Rochester. In Santa Barbara, In New Haven. Yale.

The Yale School of Music has had its share of famous faculty — Hindemith of course, and other composers of renown. And all the teachers of instruments and voice and the choruses and orchestras. As well as students.

The two most memorable visitors/celebrities I heard while at Yale were Eleanor Roosevelt, who spoke to the Yale Union of mostly men students, and Frank Lloyd Wright, who gave a speech in the architecture school. And when I returned for an occasion in the 1970s, I sat across a table from Krzysztof Penderecki and listened to a panel consisting of Aaron Copland, Penderecki and other luminaries. One gets out an autograph book at those times.

Another sidelight: two of Hindemith's teaching assistants were Mel Powell and Howard Boatwright. Powell, an eventual serialist as well as jazz artist and educator, and Boatwright, violinist/composer and early music champion were much in evidence when I was attending the Hindemith classes.

In addition to deriving much from my counterpoint classes with Hindemith and composition with Richard Donovan I had a fine piano teacher: William Gant. He was my teacher for three years and I became a much better pianist during that time and learned/memorized a fair amount of major piano literature. He was exacting, but

Emma Lou on the steps of Woolsey Hall at her graduation from the Yale School of Music

also was able to show phrase movement and expression through his gestures — the sweep of a musical line and its destination rather than just the correct notes on the correct beats. I think he also knew what kind of music fitted certain students. He had me learn several toccatas, my favorite kind of music.

Of course the most skillful teaching is done in elementary school, and junior and senior high school. Teaching in those places requires real people talent, not just a knowledge of subject.

Before leaving a discussion of Yale I should mention hearing the pipe organ rumble and shake in Woolsey Hall and the influence of Ralph Kirkpatrick on the harpsichord world — and lunch at George & Harry's and the trial runs of musicals at the Schubert Theatre and the Green where Charles Ives, once a former student, was an organist for a time in one of the churches — and the fog horns on Long Island Sound and several good friends who shared that brief, particular journey. Now onward to post-graduation life and more memories if you're still with me!....

Composer Howard Boatwright conducting the New Haven Symphony Orchestra in the late 1950s

Krzysztof Penderecki in 2008

Children in the Orchard

Music Written at Yale

Oh, maybe I should have mentioned that I wrote a lot of music at Yale. Most of it was written in one of the practice rooms or studios, either in the lower floor of the main building, where there were upright-type pianos, or in another location that I can't place. That other location had a few larger rooms and grand pianos, and in one of the rooms there was a mirror situated so that one could see a side view of one's playing — an angle I had never seen. Another side of oneself!

It was in one of those larger rooms that I did the most composing, often playing through/composing a piece and memorizing it before writing it down.

One of the works written that way was a suite for piano based on the poems in T.S. Eliot's *Landscapes*. One of the movements/poems was "Birds", another was "Children in the Orchard". Descriptive titles can set off a composer's imagination as can no other means. I believe I played the suite on a student composer recital in Sprague Hall and Hindemith heard it.

Other works for piano were two suites of three movements each and a three-movement work for two pianos titled *The Sea*, most of which was written during a Thanksgiving vacation while no one was around and I had my pick of a grand piano. I should add that these were all difficult piano works in keeping with my developing technique. A colleague, John Strauss, and I played the two-piano work at a composers conference at the New England

Conservatory. When we were rehearsing, I can remember being very particular about the way we should play it, and John at one point became a little annoyed. But we were good friends as were several other of the students I got to know.

(One of them was Donald Keats. We had some dates, one of them to a nearby amusement park where we rode the roller coaster, I screaming the whole way. Don was a fine pianist and composer, and he played fast tempos faster than anyone I knew. A few years ago we began to correspond via email, a pleasant renewal of friendship, until his death not long ago.)

There was also a three-movement violin sonata that I wrote and played with a colleague at Richard Donovan's home (he would invite his students to come occasionally and share their new pieces).

At the same place a singer performed a rather dramatic setting of mine of Psalm 137 ("By the rivers of Babylon…". My mother happened to be visiting and Professor Donovan asked if she knew her daughter could be so dramatic. (I think she said "yes").

And there was a jolly *Suite for Two Violins*. A fun piece to write, with no piano to rely on. (I just recently, seventy years later, during the pandemic, wrote a work for Philip Ficsor for two violins and viola. One of the movements is based on "Happy Days Are Here Again".)

And I wrote a work for piano and chamber orchestra, *Andante and Allegro*. It is lost. It won an award of some kind at the end of my last year.

A class assignment had us write a set of choral pieces and I chose some women poets and found that setting texts is one of the easiest things a composer can do. The school chorus read through them. It was nearly my first foray into choral writing.

Among the music written at Yale is perhaps some of my best writing. There is a tinge of Hindemith here and there, but as is often the case with composers and writers in their late teens/early twenties, there is imagination, versatility, freedom of expression and style and daring, so to speak, if I may say so as an objective observer.

I've always written a lot of music, for better or worse.

**The Brussels Conservatoire
where Emma Lou studied on a Fullbright Scholarship**

**Emma Lou playing at a high school in Brussels, Belgium, 1953 while
studying in Europe at the Brussels Conservatoire**

After Yale, Fulbright in Belgium

Have you noticed that when you have just graduated from a university or college, you believe your mind is clearer than it ever was or may never again be? As though you could accomplish anything you wanted to do? I felt that way for awhile after graduating from Yale.

My piano technique had made leaps and bounds and I thought, unrealistically really, that I might be a concert pianist. The previous year I had given a recital in Hendricks Hall at the college in Warrensburg, and another one right after graduation. It included Prokofiev's *7th Sonata* and I was learning his *3rd Piano Concerto*. I entered a regional competition for pianists and did well except for being too outside the box in the Mozart. Fortunately, I did not win, and decided the life of a composer was still my calling.

I was back home with my family and had a few piano pupils and played in a church in Kansas City (a Baptist church — Wornall Road Baptist — where the organist had a clear view of the baptisms taking place in the baptismal pool a few yards away.). I drove between Warrensburg and KC and spent a day or two in KC.

I applied for a Fulbright Scholarship to study composition and piano at the Paris Conservatoire and was accepted but as an alternate. Richard Donovan, my former teacher at Yale, urged me to apply again the next year but for the Brussels Conservatoire where there was less competition and from where I could always travel to Paris some to study there.

Along with the application I sent a vinyl (!) recording of my *Sonata in One Movement*, written at Yale, and some of the Prokofiev sonata, and was accepted. (As it turned out, I never took lessons at the Paris Conservatoire and am one of the few American composers who never studied with Nadia Boulanger, it seems.)

I voyaged over the ocean to Le Havre and by train to Paris and on to Brussels. I stayed with a Belgian family in Uccle, a suburb of Brussels, and auditioned for the Conservatoire, playing a page or so of a late Beethoven sonata before I was stopped, and admitted. My piano teacher was Andre Dumortier and I studied composition with Jean Absil, whose music I played in several recitals arranged by the Fulbright office. I wrote a symphony and some piano pieces during that period and reveled in the noon concerts and symphony concerts that had a series devoted to contemporary music.

One rainy day I was waiting for a bus to take me into Brussels and out of the fog appeared Marshall Stone, a fellow Fulbrighter who was studying organ with Flor Peeters, whose organ chorale settings surely every organist has played. I was invited to go along with Marshall to Monsieur Peeters' home and met the gracious, tall (well, everyone is tall to me) composer. I believe he had in his house an organ console that Cesar Franck had played.

At the Conservatoire I took a class in fugue writing, and remember that my offering elicited the comment "*ce n'est pas une fugue*". I've written many fugues since, but my own kind of fugue, not a strict Bach fugue, and have no regrets at all.

During that year there were vacation trips to London and Paris where I sat next to Marcel Dupré on the organ bench at St. Sulpice (hasn't everyone?) and listened to his thundering improvisation during mass in that echoing space (while we play timidly during Communion in ours).

My parents came over with a tour and I returned to the States with them first class on the *SS United States* (a new ocean liner at that time). One thing, one of the many things I missed about being in Belgium, was the pastries....

French organist and composer Marcel Dupré with whom Emma Lou sat while he improvised on the organ bench at St. Sulpice in Paris

Tacoma

When I returned to the U.S. from the Fulbright and the Brussels Conservatoire, it was necessary to have a job. I had registered with a teacher placement agency and had some notices of positions. (Incidentally, many years later it was through that agency that I learned of the vacancy at UCSB! I'll tell about that happy event eventually, if after all the years someone is still reading this).

One of the notices of vacancies was about an opening in Tacoma, Washington and the position involved teaching piano and organ, playing for chapel services and for dance classes. So I applied for that job at Annie Wright Seminary and spent an academic year in the high school division of a seminary for boys and girls. The faculty were congenial and the director/head mistress, Ruth Jenkins, was a gem of an administrator (who was not happy when I left her faculty; she moved to California after she retired and I imagine she was efficiently in charge of some organization in her later years).

I played for Nancy Barr's dance classes. Nancy had been a student of Martha Graham, so it was fun to watch the imaginative movements she and her students created while I improvised at the piano. The drama teacher put on a musical play about the seven deadly sins and I wrote music for it — intriguing to describe pride, envy, wrath, sloth, greed, gluttony and lust in music. The dance teacher provided visual interpretations. It was the closest I've come to anything theatrical, being pretty much a "purist" in the Brahms canon.

While in Tacoma I wrote a piano quartet and an orchestral suite. And a movement of my symphony that was written in Belgium was performed by the Seattle Symphony. I remember coming into the rehearsal and hearing for the first time something I had written for orchestra. It was somewhat eerie, a bit foreign. A few years later what I wrote in that medium sounded exactly as I had imagined. It's all in the practice and the experience, I think. Composers should have a good idea of the aural result of what they write, but I don't think that is always the case. There must be many instances of "I wonder what this will sound like?", "Will this be totally ineffective when it is all put together?", "Oh, did I write that?".

Composers-in-residence with an orchestra have a "guinea pig" right there, as do those associated with a choral group. I think of Vivaldi, and Haydn....

In spite of the view of Mt. Rainier, and the sightings of boats on Puget Sound and the smell of the paper mills — and the nice people — I needed to move on, and at the end of the school year I flew back to Missouri to prepare for a six-week adventure as a composition student at Tanglewood, the Berkshire Music Center in Massachusetts. And the Boston Symphony, Aaron Copland and Leonard Bernstein, et al.

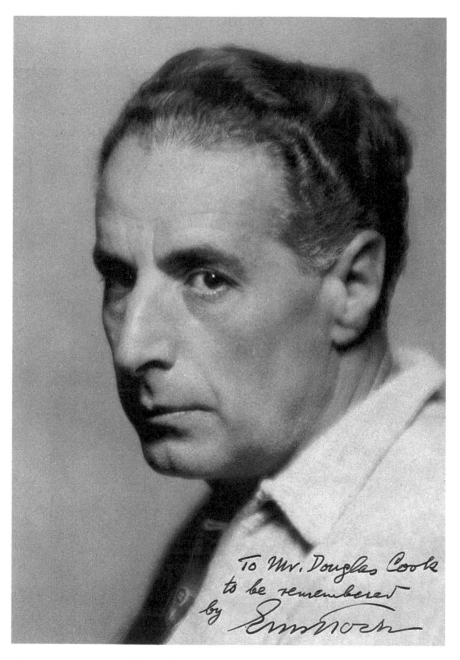

To Mr. Douglas Cook
to be remembered
by Ernst Toch

Austrian composer Ernst Toch who taught composition at the Berkshire Music Center in Massachusetts and was Emma Lou's instructor

Tanglewood

I believe it was at the opening of the term at Tanglewood that the entire student body stood and sang Randall Thompson's "Alleluia". I remember standing next to a voice major, and when you are next to a real singer, you imagine that you, too, have an excellent voice which in my case has never been true. Several hundred voices singing in perfect tune *a cappella*? It was a well-remembered experience.

I spent two summer sessions studying composition at Tanglewood (the Berkshire Music Center in Massachusetts) and my contrary nature had me choose for a teacher Ernst Toch the first summer and Roger Sessions the second summer, instead of Aaron Copland who is arguably America's most important classical composer.

We had our classes in one of the cottages, very open, plenty of fresh air. Ernst Toch, in one session, played his huge piano arrangement of a scene from Wagner — "Ride of the Valkyries" and Toch, like many composers, was an excellent pianist. In our private session he liked the short, not difficult pieces I had written "for children" — quite a contrast to the grandeur of Wagner. He (Toch) was a gracious presence, and when the symphony played one of his works, I watched him go up and be recognized, his white hair and somewhat stooped appearance somehow moving.

Roger Sessions was also a sympathetic, observant teacher, grasping easily the structure of a piece I was working on and observing that I seemed to be always heading musically for something (and not getting there?).

Aaron Copland met with the student composers a few times and he heard one of the movements of my symphony, a rather innocuous tarantella-type piece that I doubt he was overwhelmed with. I can't remember that he said anything about it, but I remember that his attitude was one of benevolence, always comforting for young composers.

The Boston Pops setting up to play "Film Night at Tanglewood" under the direction of John Williams at Tanglewood in Lenox, Massachusetts

He and Lukas Foss played several four-hand pieces together on one program, with much frivolity and fun. And later on, when I was teaching at the U. of Maryland, I believe, and having a class listen to the orchestra and soprano work *Time Cycle* by Foss, I thought back to that program at Tanglewood and one of the A.E. Housman poems he set to music:

> *When the bells justle in the tower*
> *The hollow night amid,*

Sheet music for "Toccata for Marimba" which was written by Emma Lou while at Tanglewood

Then on my tongue the taste is sour
Of all I ever did.

Leonard Bernstein gave a talk on writing the music score for *On the Waterfront*, and bemoaning how for one scene he had written a complicated fugue that was so drowned out by dialogue that it couldn't be heard. I remember Bernstein talking just a few feet before me and how blue his eyes were, at least I remember that his eyes were that color. I never got his autograph or spoke with him (Young people are so very dumb; now I would have the courage, the presumption.)

Of course the Boston Symphony enveloped the entire six weeks with monumental works like the *Berlioz Requiem* and *Harold in Italy*, performed in the "Shed", the large outdoor concert space where the audience could listen from the grassy areas or sit inside under the spacious canopy.

And I watched Charles Munch at a smaller venue close his eyes while conducting one work and seem to almost go to sleep, his baton moving slower and slower. But his conducting of the *Requiem* and other big works in the outdoor "Shed" was beyond belief in its dynamism.

During one of the summer sessions I met a percussionist who encouraged me to write a piece for marimba, which I did after returning home, and it was my first published work, "Toccata for Marimba".

Can you believe that after six weeks of luscious, rich, full orchestral sound each summer it was enough for awhile?

My favorite time was being assigned a cabin with a piano in the woods, isolated from other cabins where other composers were working, and the complete concentration that was possible there, to write music.

Kansas City
and the Death of My Father

The summer studies at Tanglewood were interspersed with winters in the Kansas City area teaching a day a week in three different colleges and playing in a church, Central Presbyterian. My parents had come to Tanglewood that last summer and it was almost the last trip that my father would take.

When I was at Yale, he came to see me there, and in a few hours he had figured out the layout of the campus and which direction was East and which was West—something I hadn't thought much about — and he recruited one of the piano majors for his college faculty back in Missouri.

When a *Suite for Orchestra* that I had entered in a Louisville Student Composers competition won first prize, it was written up in the paper "woman composer first to win orchestra prize", something like that, and I remember my parents driving to church with a look of special pride on their faces and I felt pride in their thinking their daughter had received some recognition.

My father heard the recording of the piece and thought it was great music.

Why is there a feeling of guilt in knowing that whatever one had accomplished is not very much, not enough to justify your parents' faith in you? It may be that you spend the rest of your life trying to "feel worthy" of that faith, but knowing that one's talent is not as great as Bach's or Mozart's or almost anyone else's.

But there is a philosophy, a truism, that if one sets one's goals very high and does not achieve that height, one has

Emma Lou's Father, George Willis Diemer, walking on the porch of Selmo Park in the 1940s while president of Central Missouri State College in Warrensburg, Missouri

still gone further than if one didn't have such high goals in the first place

Also, I've never had negative thoughts while writing music and continue to have joy in writing it.

But my father's health failed and he died soon after retiring from the college. He was to have been in charge of the college branch southeast of Kansas City, but that was not to be.

We had moved back to KC and my mother and grandmother and I lived in the new house, and my sister and family had built a house next door.

I wrote a cantata for my church and set many of my sister's poems to music and drove during the week to Park College and William Jewell College and the KC Conservatory to teach piano and organ and theory and probably entered a few composition contests which I usually didn't win. I had some anthems published, my first publications in that field even though I had wanted to have my piano music published because it was better music (I think my mother felt the same way), and I was happy to be with my family, always the "cocoon" that most people are grateful for.

But of course it was not enough. I grew tired of driving between schools and teaching and decided to pursue a doctorate in composition. My grandmother Casebolt was overjoyed and helped me some financially. And I applied to Eastman for admission to the Ph.D. program....

A page from ELD's dissertation at Eastman

Returning to Eastman
for a Ph.D.

W hen I returned to Eastman to work on a Ph.D. in composition, it felt quite different to be a graduate student than when eleven years earlier I was a Freshman and seventeen years old and a bit awed by the great music school (but not irreparably awed).

I chose the Ph.D. program instead of the D.M.A., one reason being that I didn't feel confident to present the required lecture recitals.

The pattern when I entered as a doctoral student was to study the first year with Bernard Rogers and the second year with Howard Hanson.

One of Bernard Rogers' orchestral works is *Elegy in Memory of Franklin D. Roosevelt*, written after FDR's death in 1945. It has the intensity of Samuel Barber's *Adagio for Strings*, though the latter was not an elegy as far as I know. (It would be interesting in another article to contemplate why one musical work becomes well-known while thousands of others do not. Is it repetition of hearing? Concisement of ideas? Simplicity even? There are many reasons.)

Rogers was a fine orchestrator and a congenial teacher.

How does one teach composition? Hanson once asked Béla Bartók to be on the Eastman composition faculty but Bartók declined because he thought it was impossible to teach composition; he would have joined the piano faculty but there were no vacancies.

Professor Rogers listened to a rather big organ piece ("Fantasie") I was writing and that I played for him on the piano. And I also wrote *Concerto for Harpsichord and Chamber Orchestra* that my notes say I premiered with Howard Hanson conducting the Eastman-Rochester Symphony Orchestra, but believe that might have been a public "reading" that Hanson conducted for many student works. Of course Hanson's skill was so immense that he could conduct a score that he had barely looked at and understand without pondering. There was one place in my piece where he immediately recognized the intent and revised his conducting mid-stream.

Dr. Bernard Rogers, composer and teacher, who taught at Eastman and was Emma Lou's doctorate instructor.

I wrote while studying with Professor Rogers a *Sonata for Flute and Harpsichord* that David Gilbert and I premiered at one of the student concerts and that has since been recorded.

That first year of the doctorate was a rather "neoclassic" period of writing for me. For some reason it was Professor Rogers' impersonal approach that brought out that element.

Howard Hanson's demeanor was totally different.

There is often that tug of war between "neoclassic" and "romantic" style in using all the musical elements. Objective, subjective, etc.

In Dr. Hanson's class, my second year at Eastman, there were about eight of us — one other woman, Gloria Swisher — and I don't remember any private lessons. Hanson's dog was there part of the time, and Dr. Hanson told us his dog preferred Mozart.

We were all writing our dissertations, orchestral works, and he had us make a two-piano version that two of us played while he followed the orchestra score.

An assignment I especially liked was to write a piece that changed from one key to another and another, etc., without modulating. Prokofiev does this and it is one of my favorite devices.

My dissertation, *A Symphony Based on American Indian Themes*, afforded a big leap in orchestration, for me, and the second movement won an Arthur Benjamin award for "quiet music".

One day Dr. Hanson told us of the Young Composers Project that the Ford Foundation and the Music Educators National Conference were sponsoring to place young composers in school systems throughout the country. It sounded exciting — and I applied....

Professor Wayne Barlow recording music

Composer in the Arlington, Virginia Schools

I finished up, completed work on, the doctorate at Eastman, having spent hours making outlines of the Gleason outlines in music history, pages of notes and studying/memorizing facts for the written exams on which I did just fine, I think. I had also to write an analysis of my dissertation, and found it quite interesting — to analyze one's own work: "Oh, I did that?", "I developed it that way?", etc. The oral exam was with Howard Hanson, Wayne Barlow, and some others. It went ok. I waited in the hall, and believe it was Professor Wayne Barlow, my thesis advisor, who told me soon after that they figured I knew more than I told them. (I wasn't a voluble talker then or now). So I passed and became Dr.

Back in Kansas City, at home, I prepared to drive to Arlington, Virginia with my mother.

I had been accepted into the Young Composers Project, the one woman in the group of twelve that first year. (At our orientation the project's director, Norman Dello Joio, addressed us as "you men") and the Music Educators National Conference (MENC)/Ford Foundation committee placed me in the secondary schools of Arlington, outside Washington, D.C.. I think they thought that would be a good fit because the two music supervisors in Arlington County were women: Florence Booker, music supervisor/choral supervisor, and Dorothy Baumle, instrumental supervisor.

2

For Mary Lou Alexander and the Girls Chorus
of Washington-Lee High School, Arlington, Virginia

Fragments from the Mass

SSAA *a cappella*

Total Duration: 5 min. 50 sec.   EMMA LOU DIEMER

Duration: 50 sec.

Kyrie

© Copyright MCMLXI by Piedmont Music Company Inc.
Sole Selling Agent: EDWARD B. MARKS MUSIC CORPORATION
International Copyright Secured   Printed in U. S. A.   All Rights Reserved
14433 - 11

There were three senior high schools and six junior high schools, and I would also write two or three pieces of music for the elementary school children.

My mother and I shopped for a used car, I having sold the one I had in Rochester which had begun to shake a lot. The $250 and a little help from my dear grandmother saw me through the last weeks of the doctorate. My mother spotted a 1957 pink Bel Air Chevy in the showroom of a used car dealer and we bought it, and a few days later drove from Kansas City to Arlington, I keeping the speed at no faster than 55, which made my mother very happy.

We stayed at the Marriott motel at Key Bridge, in sight of D.C. across the Potomac. We visited a friend of my mother and soon after met the music supervisors for lunch.

When the school year began, I was introduced to the music faculties of the various schools. Florence Booker's secretary offered me a place to stay with her and her family and it was in their home that I did much of the composing that first year.

I would visit the schools and play and talk about music I had written earlier, showing the students an orchestra or choral score and discussing it a bit.

The teachers who were most eager for music to be written for them were the choral teachers, so the first works I wrote were for SATB (soprano, alto, tenor, and bass) and SSA and TTBB, mostly with piano. I looked for texts and chose poems that were generally upbeat and youthful.

I had shown Florence Booker the choral pieces I had written at Yale and she was not enthralled, and I realized that I must not write music that was disagreeably and unnecessarily dissonant or too extreme in any way. Actually, this was not a bad thing because the purpose of the project was to write new repertoire for the schools and my aim became to find ways to make the music enjoyable to myself as well as the students. So I injected more rhythm into the writing and introduced chords that were probably new to them and that would get their attention. And I usually added piano (because, at that time, I found constant *a cappella* music a little dull).

But in this vein, one work was *Fragments from the Mass*, *a cappella*, with quite a bit of syncopation and changing meters, and the director of the girls chorus, Mary Lou Alexander, was shaking when she saw the music, but she learned it and taught it to her chorus; it is still in the repertoire, I believe.

I rebelled a bit at writing so much choral music and Dorothy Baumle asked me to write some pieces for her 100-piece orchestra. Among them was "Rondo Concertante" and another was *Symphonie Antique*. Arlington had been chosen because of the quality of that orchestra and the 100-voice chorus that Florence Booker conducted.

I wrote a suite for band (*The Brass Menagerie*) and a work for brass and percussion ("Declamation"), and a woodwind quintet. And more choral music, about which I'll talk some more....

My Time in Arlington and D.C. While Composing

The Washington area is such a great place to live for awhile. Everyone should spend weeks/months there. The first time I walked into the East Gallery of the National Gallery of Art I was transfixed, blown away by the space and the beauty. There is a wonderful echo in the East Garden Court where concerts take place and that gallery and the Washington National Cathedral must be the favorite destinations of many people, at least they are mine.

I had some pieces, works performed in the East Gallery, one of them being my dissertation, a symphony, and the critic who wrote about it was not full of praise. My mother was visiting at the time and I could see on her face that she was thinking ahead to all the disappointments and letdowns that would probably come.

But there were other concerts and other reactions and one does not stop all endeavors because of one person's opinion. My mother would appreciate the Eleanor Roosevelt quote: "No one can make you feel inferior without your consent."

I was continuing to write music for the Arlington schools and enjoying the association with the teachers who were helping their students learn new music written for them. Florence Booker, the music supervisor/choral conductor extraordinaire, said I should write some madrigals. So I looked for light, uncomplicated, enticing texts and decided on three by Shakespeare, and one afternoon set them to music.

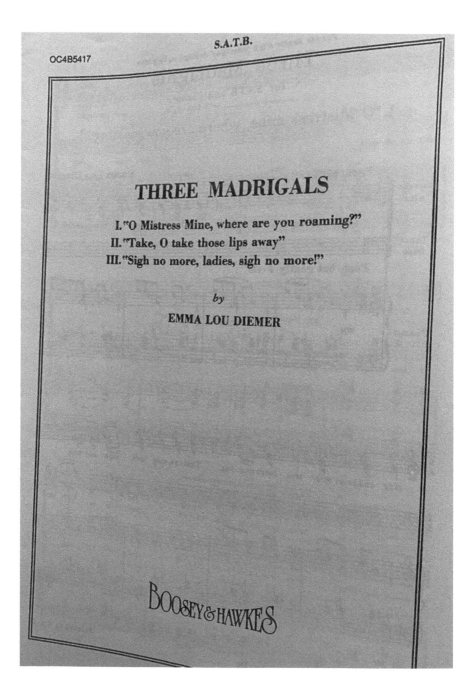

I remember the school concert when they were first sung with myself playing the piano. Audiences in Arlington had a habit of applauding whenever the music stopped, especially between movements, and after the first madrigal they were not sure because it ends up in the air with an unresolved broken chord. So their applause was hesitant. They were pretty sure when the second one ended and definitely knew when to clap after the third.

(My epitaph should read "She wrote the *Three Madrigals*") No regrets there. We composers are happy that any of our music is liked and lasts for a time. Aren't we?

The best part of composing is to come upon an idea spontaneously and hear it spin out and evolve naturally and easily, and qualify to be written down. Of course some types of music are more complicated and need to be worked with more intensely.

One can often tell when a composer has run out of good ideas and really should stop. Or if he/she has labored too hard and lost any spontaneity or intuition.

Even with a composer as prolific as Bach there are works that stand out in their unique beauty. There is no other composer who was so uniformly perfect, but still he must have had moments of unusual inspiration, and we can hear it. And in a symphonic work one waits for the most sublime moment when a certain melody or series of chords emerges from more nondescript material and shines. And the composer is aware of those moments, and may wonder where they came from.

When you write for young people, you try to write something that is memorable, catchy, alive, not mundane, lifeless. Those qualities that are in a popular song can be found in music outside the popular field, too. But there is a fine line between writing music that is trite and music that is not.

I spent two years as composer-in-residence in the Arlington schools and most of what I wrote was published. Being a composer full-time for a short span of time was priceless.

At the end of the two years I branched out again stylistically and wrote some more adventurous music. I became organist in a church on Capitol Hill and wrote music for the choir and soloists there and in time I was asked to join the composition faculty at the University of Maryland and was back in the teaching mode. Good things came of that and I'll write about them, but much happened before the new teaching stint....

Teaching in Arlington

After the two-year residency in the Arlington schools and before teaching at the University of Maryland things were quite unsettled. My grandmother, who had lived with us all my life, died before I finished the doctorate. I've written about her and the other members of my close family in earlier stories. She was ninety, and had been a guiding force.

Florence Booker wanted to keep me in the Arlington school system and she had arranged for some teaching for me in two of the schools, and the MENC had asked me to do some consulting in the Baltimore schools as part of the Contemporary Music Project, which involved visiting classes and bringing contemporary ideas of rhythm and scales to the teachers and children.

I went back home in the summers; and in the last summer, 1961, after the Arlington residency, I was to see my mother at home for the last time.

I had just begun teaching a general music class in one of the junior high schools when my brother phoned to tell me our mother was in the hospital. I flew home, feeling as though the world was becoming quite a sad and lonely place. Her little dog was waiting outside the house, waiting for my mother to return.

We gathered at the hospital every day and finally had to say farewell. I remember that at the cemetery in Warrensburg I felt like an orphan, which I was, at thirty-three.

I went back to Arlington for a not very successful few weeks teaching in the junior high school. In my general music class there was a majority of bright, interested young people but also a few who were noisy and not enthralled when I talked about music. However, when I sat down and played the piano for them (pieces like Debussy's "Golliwog's Cake Walk"), they were quiet, really a bit transfixed by the music. There are teachers who keep their students' attention without playing the piano. I was not one of them.

The following summer, alone for the day in the house in KC, I wrote a boisterous piece for the Arlington school orchestras ("Festival Overture"), a parting commission for the school system. I can remember pounding out the rhythmic score and seeing out the window a neighbor walking by on the road and looking at our house, probably wondering what wild and jazzy music that was.

I arranged for the house to be rented and the piano to be moved to Arlington and took our blue parakeet in a hat box and flew back to Virginia. My sister and brother-in-law and their four children were moving to Huntsville, Alabama, taking with them my mother's little Pekingese, so our two houses would soon have other occupants.

The flutist, Mark Thomas, asked me to write a flute concerto for him to play with the Omaha Symphony and there was great joy in doing that. Flying over Kansas on the way to Omaha for the premiere I was aware that my wonderful brother, John, who had become an administrator in the footsteps of our father, was ill and here I was flying off for a premiere. John died soon after, and again I left Virginia to be for a few days with Lois, my sister-in-law, and their four children.

There was more music to come, and happenings in our country that made this period well-remembered, not to mention chaotic as well as sorrowful and sometimes joyful....

For Mark Thomas

CONCERTO
For Flute and Orchestra (1963)

I

By EMMA LOU DIEMER

* s.p.= sostenuto pedal. Pedal normally where special pedaling is not indicated. ✱ = s.p. or pedal off.

Exterior of the Lutheran Church of the Reformation in Washington, D.C. where Emma Lou was the organist while teaching in the area

Organist for
Reformation Lutheran and
Music for Kindler Commission

I was living in an apartment in Arlington, doing some teaching in the schools there and in Baltimore and also had been organist in two different Arlington churches (one a Presbyterian church and the other, Resurrection Lutheran) when I had a call one day from Elizabeth Boos, organist at Reformation Lutheran in Washington, D.C.. She said she wanted me to audition for the job since she was leaving.

The music program was directed by Jule and Peggy Zabawa, and I remember (after I became organist) sitting at the organ and listening to the choir sing a Bach chorus *a cappella* with such precision and accuracy. The Zabawas were St. Olaf graduates and devotees of the *vibrato*-less singing voice, one advantage of which is more transparent counterpoint.

The church was a block or two from the Supreme Court and across the street from the Folger Shakespeare Library. I played at Reformation nine years, driving in from Virginia two or three times a week. Sometimes I returned on a Sunday afternoon to have some of the best practices I ever had, alone in that quiet, subdued space.

Also about that time I was commissioned by the Kindler Foundation to write a work for *Piano and Woodwind Quintet*. I believe Richard Bales, conductor of the National Gallery orchestra (which had played my symphony to no great acclaim), was an instigator in the commission.

I would come home from doing some teaching and dive into the composing, not really aware of a nice older couple in a nearby apartment or the parking lot outside the window. I listened to a Wallingford Riegger work in that medium and thought "I can do better than that", or actually the motivation was to write for the medium in my own way.

It was a three-movement work, and Emerson Myers played the piano in the premiere. A reviewer was generally pleased, though he wrote of the "relentless energy that never lets up." One could say that of a great deal of music. A composer often writes with that level of enthusiasm. Did Bach ever not?

The work, if I may be allowed to critique it, was a major effort, and should be in the repertoire. (How many times has a composer thought that of her/his composition?)

Another phone call I had was from Homer Ulrich at the University of Maryland. He asked me to teach piano and organ a day a week at the university, which I did for a year and then was asked to join the theory/composition faculty. I had by that time bought a small house in Falls Church, in Fairfax County, about a mile from the 495 beltway, and I drove to Silver Spring several times a week....

My Time with the University of Maryland

So I began the three-headed existence of university professor, composer, and organist in a church. At the University of Maryland I soon became acquainted with Stewart Gordon, of the piano faculty, and wrote for him a set of seven *études* for piano.

There are times in a composer's creative life when one is so eager to write music, so finding it necessary to express somehow all that has gone before and to put into sounds the vivid impressions one has from atmospheres and events—so anxious to do this that there is a rush to get it sorted out and put on paper.

The first *étude* was a reaction, a real reaction to the Selma-Montgomery civil rights march that occurred in Alabama in 1965. How does one express anything in music? With whatever musical means one is able to. I have scarcely written any music that did not have some emotional meaning in it, and guess that is why I've never gotten excited about matrices and theories, although I've used them, but on my own terms, and never in a dispassionate way. I think it's called "academic music" when there is no "heart."

So the first *étude* was alive with rather angry declaimed chords and syncopated lines in canon, and speed and energy in the form of close-packed harmonies and wide-spread motives and...unrelenting energy.

Another *étude* was a parody of Schoenberg, not 12-tone but with leaps of line tonally disconnected and amusingly fragmented and staccato at the end.

Another had the arpeggiated bass of Rachmaninoff with a single-line melody above.

Another was thirds, everywhere, in different registers.

Another was all tremolo.

The last was a circus of dotted rhythm and contrary motion, a bit erratic and driving.

I wrote them almost all at once. As I've said before, if music-writing is spontaneous (though finally carefully worked out) and has not been labored over, but rolls out easily (with help from above or some other mysterious place of intuition), the composer has usually created something she or he, at least, can be proud of.

Stewart played them beautifully and the reviewer was ebullient. And they are in someone's cupboard and in a rental library and a young pianist has recently discovered them.

Another work that was painlessly, joyously written was "Four Chinese Love-Poems for Soprano and Harp." Audrey Nossaman, of the University of Maryland voice faculty, sang them with Steward Gordon as pianist. I can't remember the name of the harpist who first played them in the original, with another singer. She was, I believe, harpist with the National Symphony. Sylvia Meyer? She did not think it was a harp-friendly work.

I've found that when a performer complains about his/her part it is sometimes because of his/her inadequacy rather than the composer's. But the songs are probably more effective with piano.

One of the works I wrote for Reformation Lutheran, where I was organist, was a "Service in Music and Poetry." The surviving piece from that is "Dance, dance my heart", a madrigal-like choral work with piano, on a text by Kabir.

At that time in church music the "guitar masses" and jazz-inflected offerings were taking the place of traditional music in some churches. I have a memory of one of Duke Ellington's "Sacred Music Concerts" performed in the National Cathedral.

(Above) Peggy and Jule Zabawa. Church of the Reformation, Washington, D.C.

I have written some jazz-inflected organ pieces for church, some at that time.

Stravinsky conducted a concert of his own works in a half-filled Constitution Hall and I watched him leave afterward, an old man, probably our greatest composer of the century.

The Zabawas, in time, moved on to a church in Baltimore and successive choir directors were Harlan Snow (for whom I later wrote a song cycle for his degree work at Northwestern) and Vito Mason (a delightful, fine conductor and professor at American University).

I wrote many pieces/works in those years — song cycles, a cantata, more chamber music, organ music — I'll not bore you with. One Sunday, tired of playing the same setting of the service, I reharmonized it all, not forewarning the choir nor making them at all happy. Organists can be real pills.

At the university I taught counterpoint, orchestration, analysis, and composition, and had some well-remembered students including John Horman, who went on to be a treasured friend and composer.

Of course I remember exactly where I was when John Kennedy was assassinated. And when Lyndon Johnson announced that he would not run for another term. And when Martin Luther King was gunned down and the riots in Washington that followed. And the death of Robert Kennedy. And the moon landing. And the disastrous oil spill off the coast of Santa Barbara and the environmental movement that started then.

It was quite a time, my twelve years in the Washington area, but the traffic from the beltway, Lee Highway and Highway 50 became too much. It seemed to surround the Pine Spring development in Falls Church where I lived. So I was off to California with two dogs, a white Persian cat, and a blue parakeet to teach at UCSB....

Moving to California to Teach at UCSB

One should never say "This is the last place I will live", because often it isn't. I did not feel that way about the D.C./Virginia location, that it would be my final destination; and although I had a wonderful twelve years there and would miss my friends and the music and the experience of living near the nation's capital and would look back on a cherished period, it was time to move on.

I was still registered with a teacher placement agency and one of the notices was for a composition/theory position at the University of California, Santa Barbara.

I had been offered a position in New Mexico but had turned it down, and had considered some others.

I didn't know anything about Santa Barbara—someone in my church said there was a beautiful courthouse there. But I was bright enough to see that the city was on the coast and that was enough reason for me to apply.

I believe it was late in August, 1971 that I had a phone call from Peter Racine Fricker, chair of the music department at UCSB. He asked if I was still interested in the position and I said yes. I was "hired" then, on the phone.

In looking back, I wondered why, with no interview, no visit, I was offered the position. I believe it had something to do with the fact that Dr. Fricker was a supporter of women composers (he had invited Thea Musgrave to be visiting professor at times and had a strong contingent of women on the music faculty). Also, he was an organist and

Peter Fricker, English composer and chair of the music department at UCSB, who hired Emma Lou for the faculty in 1971

had written quite a bit of organ music, as had I. In addition, his secretary remembered singing my *Three Madrigals* in high school! (Here one should put a knowing smile.)

So I placed my Virginia house in the hands of the agent who had found it for me seven years earlier, and began packing the many, many boxes for the move, and early one morning saw the moving van off and departed on the cross country trip to Santa Barbara, about 2,742 miles away.

I had two little Pekingese dogs with me, a white Persian cat, and a blue parakeet, Dewdrop, that had flown into our garden at our Kansas City house some years before. He could talk quite a bit so was good company. I was worried that he might not survive the trip. He did, but a group of goldfish that I took along did not make it through a chilly night at one of the motels.

I stopped briefly in Huntsville, Alabama to see my sister Dorothy and my brother-in-law Wick and their four children.

I remember driving west through the desert and being blinded by the setting sun. I pulled over and waited until dusk, beginning to learn that headlights were necessary at all times to be warned of approaching cars and to be seen. I also noticed the light reflectors marking the space between the lanes, something I hadn't seen on the East Coast, and found these very helpful.

We (my pets and I) drove for quite some time through the crowded freeways of Los Angeles, the air not as clear as it would be in a few years.

And then, coming into Ventura on the 101 freeway, suddenly there was the Pacific Ocean, the largest ocean on Earth, and soon the city of Santa Barbara.

I think of all the movie scenes that have been made along that coast and all the tourists and movie stars that have fled to the quieter, smaller city of Santa Barbara from the immensity of Los Angeles.

I found a place to live, one of only two that welcomed pets, a townhouse in a new development up on Miramonte Drive. The development was called Santa Barbara Highlands and eventually it was extended and the dwellings converted to condominiums. But when I moved there, the townhouses were rented.

It took the visit, later, of one my nieces, Bonny, to discover that if we hiked up Miramonte to the top, there was a view of the entire harbor and the city, spread out below.

Miramonte View of Santa Barbara Harbor

My appointment to the teaching position had been a late one due to the sudden illness and retirement of my predecessor, Roger Chapman, and the fall term that year began in October. I was surprised that the evenings in Santa Barbara were cooler than they were in Missouri and Virginia. I hadn't experienced living in a Mediterranean climate until Santa Barbara.

I soon met some of my colleagues and Peter Fricker, the tall (as I've noted before, almost everyone is tall to me), distinguished British composer. And his wife, Helen, who had a varied background of music-making and a fine sense of humor.

My office, with a view from the window of the small music bowl/amphitheater in which noon concerts and sometimes theatrical performances were staged, opened out to the fresh air.

My office number was 1111. Sometime I will tell how the number eleven is found in every one of my family's birthday dates. Data that my mother told me when I was small, and seems a bit mystical.

UCSB was about ten miles from the city of Santa Barbara, and when I drove out from Miramonte there was a view of the mountains with dots of houses on the hillsides in the distance.

I taught an early morning theory class that first quarter, and sometimes the fog from the ocean enveloped the campus when I arrived. When I left later in the day, the bright sun was out and the ocean was to the right and the mountains, the Santa Ynez range, was to the left. It was unbelievably beautiful. I never failed to marvel at that view and eventually at almost everything about being at UCSB....

The Geiringers, Karl and Irene, Karl a distinguished musicologist at UCSB and Irene who helped him in his writing research, were special friends of Emma Lou

Karl Geiringer and
Other Faculty at UCSB

Karl Geiringer, the distinguished musicologist, was on the emeritus faculty when I moved to Santa Barbara to teach at UCSB. (Read about Dr. Geiringer in *Wikipedia* or any music history book). He was the oldest member of the faculty and the only one to take an interest in our electronic music lab. He visited it and mentioned it in his *Instruments in the History of Western Music*.

He and his wife, the brilliant Irene, who collaborated on his writings, lived up on the "Riviera", a section of Santa Barbara overlooking the harbor and the city. I passed him in my car one day and saw him climbing up that steep hill, probably writing his next book in his mind. (I didn't offer to give him a ride because it would be a bit tricky on that winding road, and also people out walking do not usually want to be picked up.)

I was a guest in the Geiringer home a few times. Karl was one of those people, like Howard Hanson, who had a generous spirit and an all-encompassing mind. There are "academics" who have a specialty and are absorbed in it, emerge to read a paper at a convention now and then and return to their research. And there are others, like the Geiringers, like Hanson, who are looking around, for more to learn.

Of course others on the faculty were equally open and alive. Dolores Hsu, another musicologist, although a bit younger than I, was a kind of mentor when I came to the university. She was a dynamic chair of the department for

Dolores Hsu, another musicologist at UCSB who was a special friend of Emma Lou

eleven years (and instituted the practice of having wine at faculty meetings — just before we all drove home...).

And there was Erno Daniel, elegant piano professor, whose wife was Katinka Daniel, well-known exponent of the *Kodaly* pedagogy method in music education. She lived a few blocks above my present house and walked down to the bus, not being a driver. She told us that the Russians had broken her fingers when her native Hungary was occupied during the second world war. Her husband preceded her to the United States and it was several years before she could join him.

In another essay I mentioned all the faculty for whom I wrote music. There were several, and the music written for them was some of which I am most proud....

Life in Santa Barbara
and UCSB

After a few years living on the Mesa I moved to San Antonio Village, a condominium development a little closer to the university and where I could buy a house (actually half of a duplex) rather than pay rent.

The least expensive dwelling there, at that time, was $25,000. If I had a lot of money, I could have bought several and become a millionaire in a few years, what with the present high prices of homes in Santa Barbara.

There was a bike path nearby, and Marilyn and I (Marilyn Skiöld, who had left Sweden and come to live with me in 1978) would bike all the way, along Goleta Beach, to the university or stop at the beach and have a picnic. Those were the days I could bike for some distance, against the wind. A long time ago.

At that time the engineering building was the most prominent building on campus; now there are dozens more new buildings and about fifteen thousand more students and bicycles.

Also, at that time, students sometimes brought their dogs to class.

The university remained an exciting place, and there was a diversity to the music that was created there.

One of the students, Marc Ream, lined up everyone around the seats in Lotte Lehmann Concert Hall, lined them up at the far sides, and gave them a few notes to sing at different times — surround sound.

Living in Santa Barbara, on Chino Street, was Henry Brant, one of the composers who wrote many works for large spaces like the very modern St. Mary's Cathedral in San Francisco.

Brass and pipe organs have been very popular with composers, not to mention voices, for volume and spatial effectiveness. Of course early composers like the Gabrielis and Monteverdi wrote music for antiphonal brass and voices, making use of the space and acoustics of St. Mark's in Venice.

Electronic music composers placed speakers in different locations for spatial effects. Choir directors in their churches liked to spread the voices in the side aisles. Organs had antiphonal divisions for contrast.

These various new and old ways of creating music are more innovative, I think, than the serialists, the Schoenberg spin-offs whose music evolved from European composers. Twelve-tone matrixes and "set theory" had become king. Along with the use of space that composers like Marc Ream and Henry Brant explored, coupled with the resurgence, the intimations of tonality within minimalism, made for a different kind of expression that I think, in my less-then-erudite way, was a more "romantic" way of writing music. Adventurous. Freer. Less academic. I'm not a music historian or music theorist. Just a composer. Those of you who are historians/theorists/musicologists can expound tediously on the subject.

My favorite sound on campus is the carillon in Storke Tower. It has sixty-one bells and on the hour plays a musical adaptation of the university motto *Fiat lux* — "Let there be light". If there is anyplace on Earth where there should be light, it is a university where students and faculty learn and teach....

Counterpoint, Teaching at UCSB, and the Electronic Studio

I love counterpoint, and at UCSB I taught sixteenth century and eighteenth century counterpoint (Bach). I preferred eighteenth century because it was largely instrumental rather than strict choral writing that had rule upon rule of voice movement. But there are "rules", harmonic principles in Bach. There will not be found a chord structure that is not built on thirds — at least not one that is not resolved. And the lines move as if driven by some inner force.

When I was much younger and listening to an organ fugue, I could recognize the subject when it appeared, but I would be lost in the material in between. When one begins to study and play a fugue, one learns what all that material is, and if the composer is like Bach, it is all related and can be analyzed.

We studied all the devices in fugue-writing: inversion, augmentation, diminution, retrograde, subject, countersubject, episode, *stretto*. My favorite is augmentation when (on the organ) the subject's statement is in long notes in the pedal with busy development going on above.

When I was working on the doctorate at Eastman, there was a class that I enjoyed taught by theorist Allen McHose. He asked us to write pieces "in the style of" various composers, so we wrote — tried to write — like Schumann or Brahms or some other distinctive composer.

Of course what we wrote never sounded exactly like the model, but we had to study the way the composer used the elements of music and imitate them. Imitation is how young composers begin. But if one goes through life imitating someone else, there is not much creativity.

At UCSB we studied Bach counterpoint using Kent Kennan's book and I had the students sing the inventions and fugues, not just look at them. It was good practice for me, playing them at the piano, and it allowed the students to participate and be surrounded by the wonders of counterpoint while struggling with all the16th notes.

"Teaching" composition is another conundrum. One good thing about UCSB at that time was that the four composition teachers each wrote in different styles. Peter Fricker's music was often atonal and demanding, Edward Applebaum (who joined the department at the same time I did) was closer to being a serialist than the rest of us, JoAnn Kuchera-Morin (who came to UCSB a few years later) wrote complicated, denser tonalities, and I was more eclectic. Interesting that there were two men and two women on the composition faculty at that time, perhaps never again to have that equality.

My class of a few students in beginning composition met in my office, as did private lessons, and I assigned projects like writing an extended melodic line, a piece, for some instrument, using motives that were developed and that had an overall shape or structure. Another was to write a theme and variations — their favorite — with contrasts of texture and even tonality.

Other classes were in orchestration, with much study of scores and much listening (how else does one "learn" orchestration?), and contemporary analysis.

Before I left the Washington area in 1971 and moved to California, I went to Emerson Myers' workshops at Catholic University in tape music, electronic music. It was an effort to force myself to break away from traditional timbres and means of expression.

(Top) Emma Lou at the electronic studio/computer in her home where she often composed and digitized her sheet music

(Bottom) Emma Lou using synthesizers and tapes for composing

So at UCSB when we were offered creative arts grants to develop new programs, I, with a graduate student's help, started an electronic music lab complete with several synthesizers. Keyboard synthesizers were being developed, and that interested me more than the plugging in of patch cords and twirling dials.

Working in that medium (I acquired a series of synthesizers to work on at home) changed my style of writing for acoustic instruments somewhat. More advanced students and JoAnn Kuchera-Morin carried on that enterprise into computer music writing and to much greater heights....

Emma Lou showing the medal she was presented as retiring faculty at University of California Santa Barbara

Last Years
Of Teaching at UCSB

The 1980s were my last years of teaching at UCSB, and the very last year was 1990-91. However, the spring quarter of that year was a sabbatical quarter, so I didn't teach after the winter quarter. I have kept my grade books, green spiral-bound records, so can bring to mind most of the students from those years, and there were many outstanding ones. Some of them are still in town, but I wouldn't dare to mention any in particular for fear of leaving someone out.

I have never claimed to be a brilliant teacher. My talents, for whatever they are worth, have been in making music at the keyboard and transcribing it to manuscript paper or computer, in other words, a keyboard performer/composer — with university teaching as an occupation.

Being a professor at UCSB was an honor, a learning experience, a chance to meet a lot of talented young people. If ever I had some worth as a professor, it was being able to study their scores and read through them at the piano during sessions and make comments that might prove helpful.

In the later years I didn't teach many classes; it was mostly a one-on-one "lesson" which I enjoyed very much, but being in front of a class can also be "fun", a chance to "perform" in front of a group (and don't tell me teachers do not like that role).

And I think of Peter Fricker, who was the department chair who "hired" me on the phone and was such an admirable friend and colleague for those twenty years. About a year before he died, Peter was unable to speak, I believe because of throat cancer, but he continued to meet with his students, communicating by writing his comments for them to read and still probably illustrating, playing at the piano. I visited him in the hospital, and he had music paper at hand, waiting to be covered with his notes, his musical thoughts.

I mentioned in a previous "story" of going on campus earlier this year, just at the beginning of the awareness, the outbreak of the coronavirus, the place deserted and quiet. And I visited it not long ago, masked of course, and walked by the offices, mine just off the music bowl. There was no music "echoing in the halls" — I don't have that vivid a recall in imagination — but there were memories of playing and listening in Lotte Lehmann Concert Hall, waiting in the many-mirrored dressing room down below before a concert.

And Storke Plaza with the carillon, that giant instrument (the biggest producer of music in the whole county — although it can barely be heard beyond the borders of the campus, but my first experience of sound at UCSB).

And the other "place of business", the church where I played for a number of years, these days closed and empty, the organ waiting to come to life and resound again.

So much for nostalgia, now back to the music... next...a lot happened in the 1990s, and since....

**Storke Plaza at UCSB and the tower
which houses the beautiful carillon bells**

SECTION THREE
Composing and for Whom

Piano Reduction

Concerto in One Movement
for Marimba and Orchestra

Emma Lou Diemer
marimba ed. by
Deborah Schwartz

Brilliant, Spirited ♩ = C. 108

Marimba

Piano

Big Works

The rise and fall and rise again (?) of big works. We composers feel most proud, perhaps, of the larger compositions we have brought forth. Larger in terms of forces and duration. That includes concertos, symphonies, operas. Sonatas and such can be big, too, but the number of performers it takes to perform a work seems to be the criterion of bigness, "greatness".

Big doesn't mean better any more than loud does. An organist can easily push a button and literally pull out all the stops and play a chord *fortissimo*, and people will stand in awe and admiration. I've had folks say to me, after I played a loud chord or passage, "how can such a little person make all that sound!"

And orchestra composers who use all the instruments and have them play full force (especially the brass, with percussion joining in) produce gasps of astonishment, maybe fear, also loss of hearing.

A composer can write all manner of intricate counterpoint or filigree of instrumental sensitivity, but if it isn't loud, the audience will go to sleep.

The composer learns how to create a busy, loud ending, especially in the last measures of a concerto, to rouse the listeners from their seats, clapping ferociously. So the composer can "orchestrate" a standing ovation.

A piece that ends quietly — and there are some — produces an attitude of disbelief and maybe uncertainty. Of course it can be effective too, but that isn't my point.

My point is that no matter how many small-force works you write, you may have to bring forth some *big* ones, some *loud* ones, to be considered "great".

And that brings me to the "big" compositions I've written.

My teenage wish to be a "great" composer — and I think most composers have that wish — meaning writing symphonies and concertos, which I've done. But it seems to be the smaller, shorter pieces that are performed. I don't begrudge the small pieces — I like them, too. (It is not good for a composer not to like what she/he has written!)

And I think of Chopin, who wrote mostly for piano and created some of the most beautiful pieces ever written — short ones, longer ones.

Some examples of "bigger" compositions: I wrote a multi-movement work for the San Francisco Choral Society some years ago. It was with full orchestra (what orchestra is not full? or have some degree of fullness?) and used texts by several women poets plus Omar Khayyam. It was/is what I would call a sensitive work, not avant-garde, not bombastic, not "big". It was being written at a time when my sister was beginning to lose her life to a terminal illness.

I remember composing some of it while filling in for my friend in a pet-sitting job at someone's house. I brought a synthesizer keyboard along and wrote several movements with the little dog, Kacey, sitting in a chair beside me.

During the writing of the setting of Emily Dickinson's poem "I robbed the woods" both Kacey and I were quite moved. The setting is very tonal, quiet, but intense, repetitive. Someone — the critic, I suppose—thought it didn't have much to it.

The other movements, with texts by Mary Oliver, Omar Khayyam, Hildegard von Bingen, were not world-shaking either, just expressive. Dare I say "from the heart?" The most dramatic movement used a poem by my sister, Dorothy, that spoke of earth's possible destruction because of our lack of care for it—lack of care for Earth. Actually,

I thought that was the best movement. And it was the loudest.

But the work, titled *Songs For The Earth* was coupled in the concert with *Carmina Burana*, an opus that has dogged me since I first heard it in Belgium many years before. Like Handel's *Messiah*, it is played over and over. *Messiah* is performed annually in many places and it is a magnificent composition, particularly "For unto us a child is born", which with its counterpoint and momentum would always rouse me from slumber as a child sitting through the yearly performances of *Messiah* at the college in Warrensburg.

Carmina Burana is full of rhythm, repetition, and has its charm. And my quieter, thoughtful choruses about saving the earth hadn't a chance.

The opposite happened when a lengthy movement of a *Mass* I had written, for chorus and two pianos and percussion, was performed. The "Gloria" movement, was the "winner" in the sense that it surprised the critic. Why? It was full of energy, rhythmic, *loud* in some places. The *Mass*, of which I was proud, was published and the "Agnus Dei" has a bit of shelf life, and the Donald Brinegar Singers made a recording of the whole work for the publisher's use.

I've written several concertos, for organ, for piano, flute, marimba, harpsichord. The piano concerto, which won a Kennedy Center Friedhelm award, was one long movement, and had a ferocious, *loud* ending that brought the pianist an ovation. I remember writing that ending, the *coda*, and knowing what it would cause, and feeling happy that I knew some people would like it.

Other chorus/orchestra works that I've written are "Invocation" on a poem by May Sarton (I sent her a tape and she wrote that although she couldn't hear the words she thought I had captured the meaning). And "There is a morn unseen" on an Emily Dickinson text (the original title is "There is a morn by men unseen"); it's on *YouTube* as are several works including "Nature" from *Songs For The Earth*. And *Anniversary Choruses*, a work with biblical and Southern writer texts that Don Hinshaw thought would be the composition of the year and I thought so, too, when it was performed by 400 singers and orchestra in a South Carolina auditorium. (But it wasn't.)

The composer's road is a somewhat bumpy road, but one would choose no other.

There are so many works that have taken the composer much effort to write and much joy in doing so-works that are entombed by time. But sometimes they *rise* again, and if they're *loud* enough, they will be heard....

The Concerto and I

Did you listen to (mostly) piano concertos when you were growing up? Tchaikovsky? Grieg? Gershwin? I certainly did — played the records over and over. I even had a record that had only the orchestra part for some concertos, and you could play the solo and imagine that you were playing with a live orchestra!

This story/article/memoir will be about the concertos I wrote — mainly for me to remember the circumstances, and for you to turn to other things if you don't want more "me-ness" to read about.

There are about a dozen — not quite equaling Vivaldi's 500, Mozart's 23 for piano alone. Bach's 28, the dozens by Haydn. In high school I wrote two piano concertos, one in A minor, one in G minor, and I remember working on the G minor one after finding a piano at an educators conference my father attended with my mother and myself coming along. Those concertos are lost, went missing in the move from Virginia to California long ago — a box containing manuscripts, music writing tablets lay forgotten in the back of the moving van.

I took one of the concertos which had some rudimentary orchestration to Wiktor Labunski with whom I was studying piano at the Kansas City Conservatory and he had some good suggestions about having more activity in the woodwinds, melodic imitation (I remember him pointing to the score where these could be added). I was 15.

Concerto

FOR
Flute and Orchestra
(PIANO REDUCTION BY THE COMPOSER)

BY
Emma Lou Diemer

ST-391

$15.00

SOUTHERN MUSIC COMPANY
SAN ANTONIO, TEXAS 78212

At Yale I wrote a piano and chamber work, *Andante and Allegro* and played it with the school orchestra. I remember a couple of themes from it — happy ones (a fellow student, Armin Watkins, told me it was fine to write happy music sometimes). That piece won a prize at graduation. I wish I could find it, but believe it was in the box that was lost in the aforementioned move.

In other stories I mention or discuss the later concertos I wrote for flute, harpsichord, piano (2), marimba, organ, violin. Most of them were commissioned, and all are published.

Immortal, Invisible, God Only Wise

ST. DENIO
Welsh Hymn Melody
Setting by Emma Lou Diemer

WPAL-23   ©The Sacred Music Press 1978

Simple Songs

I took away (from *Facebook*) the latest little hymn tune settings, the interest being underwhelming, although the hopeful idea of "Be Not Dismayed What E'er Betide" seemed important in this absolutely dreadful time (2020 before the election) we are surviving. The journey of a tiny owl created more interest and actually maybe more hope.

But that hymn is worth looking at again because it is one of the few that is in *triple meter* and lends itself to a lilting tempo and mood. Another that does that is "Open My Eyes, That I May See", words and music by a woman, Clara H. Scott. When I played it for church, I couldn't help giving it a light, dance-like feel.

I like big works — requiems, cantatas, masses — as well as the next person, and have written some. But a simple song maybe reaches more people. Think "Sing God a Simple Song", the Bernstein/Schwartz creation with the last line:

"For God is the simplest of all…" — quite a concept. I'm not sure I know what it means; it is mysterious like most religious ideas. And that is perhaps the beauty of religion — not to understand completely. Music has to make it more evident?

But getting back to the few hymns, church songs that are in triple meter, my favorite is "Immortal, Invisible". Its melody is of the utmost simplicity, being mostly repetitive broken chords rather than scale-wise, step-wise construction (for scale/step-wise think "Joy to the World"). Another broken-chord simple song is "Amazing Grace", probably the best-known tune in the whole world. Simple.

When you play for church, you like some hymns and really don't like some others very much. I always enjoyed playing "Immortal, Invisible", especially having it "get to me" in the verse:

> *"Unresting, unhasting, and silent as light,*
> *Nor wanting, nor wasting, thou rulest in might;*
> *We blossom and flourish as leaves on the tree,*
> *And wither and perish, but naught changeth thee."*
> *And of course I wrote an organ setting of it.*
> *Rhythm, beauty in the words and in the music.*

A Bit About Songs

You may wonder why I post/expose to view these facts and figures and stories about one's music-writing and life experiences, it being an act of egocentrism, perceived, and of no great interest outside of a few friends and a few family members.

It is because history erases most of us and sometimes obliterates all we do. Sometimes our acts of commission are rescued by a kind relative or a dedicated historian, but usually not. So one must justify one's own existence by spouting forth statistics and recording them, whether met with indifference or curiosity. And if the teeming half-dozen are waiting for more, here it is. (And remember that the "great composers" also wrote a huge amount of music — be not dismayed; if one is a composer, one composes.)

In smaller print I'll list the art songs and song cycles, both sacred and secular. I don't, unfortunately, write popular songs. Included are the text source and publisher.

VOCAL WORKS (Art Songs):

Songs of Reminiscence for Soprano and Piano, texts by Dorothy Diemer Hendry, 1958 (Seesaw, 1968).

Three Mystic Songs for Soprano and Baritone Voice and Piano, ancient Hindu texts, 1963 (Seesaw, 1968). Premiered by Peggy and Jule Zabawa, National Gallery of Art, Washington, D.C., 1963.

Four Chinese Love-Poems for Soprano and Harp or Piano, ancient Chinese texts, 1965 (Seesaw, 1976). Premiered by Audry Nossaman and Stewart Gordon, Univ. of Maryland, 1965.

The Four Seasons for Soprano or Tenor and Piano, text from *The Fairie Queen* (Spencer), 1969 (Seesaw, 1981). Premiered by Kenneth Pennington, Phillips Gallery, Washington, D.C., 1969.

Four Poems by Alice Meynell for Soprano or Tenor and Chamber Ensemble (2 flutes/ piccolo, 2 percussion, vibraphone, xylophone, harp, harpsichord, piano, strings), 1976 (Carl Fischer, 1977). (Commissioned by Mu Phi Epsilon, premiered in Kansas City, MO, 1976).

Lute Songs on Renaissance Poetry for Tenor and Piano, 1986 (Seesaw, 1988). (Commissioned by Professional Music Teachers Assoc. of California, premiered by Carl Zytowski and Emma Lou Diemer, Ventura, CA, 1986).

"I Will Sing of Your Steadfast Love" for high voice and organ. (Psalm 89). (Sisra Publications, 1984). Written for Millie Fortner, First Presbyterian Church, Santa Barbara.

"And I Saw a New Heaven and a New Earth for Medium High Voice, Trumpet, and Organ or Piano," text from Revelation 21, 1991 (Arsis Press, 1991) Premiered by Audrey Sharpe, Philip Mann, and ELD, First Presbyterian Church, Santa Barbara.

Two Songs: "Shall I Compare Thee to a Summer's Day?" (Shakespeare) and "October Wind" (Dorothy Diemer Hendry) (Southern Music Co., San Antonio, 1995; Lauren Keiser Music Publishing, 2012) in Vol. 4 of Art Songs by American Women Composers.

Four songs: "Strings in the Earth and Air" (James Joyce), "The Caller" (Dorothy Diemer Hendry), "One Perfect Rose" (Dorothy Parker), "Comment" (Parker) in *Art Songs by American Women Composers*, Vol. 14 (Southern Music Co., 2000; Lauren Keiser Music Publishing, 2012).

Three Christmas Songs for High Voice and Organ, 1994. (National Music Publishers, 2002). Premiered by Audrey Sharpe, Robert Wilke, and Mary Silver with ELD, organ, at First Presbyterian Church, Santa Barbara, CA, December, 1994. "On Christmas Night", from this cycle, is published in Karen Leigh-Post's *Anthology of American Art Songs for the Sacred Service*, pub. by Vocal Music Imprints, 2004.

"On This Wedding Day," 2002 (National Music Publishers, 2003). Text by Dorothy Diemer Hendry. Written for the wedding of Jessicah Krey and Chris Duckworth, October 2002. "Wedding Song." Text by Dorothy Diemer Hendry. Written for the wedding of Deanna Augsburger and Eddie Burwell, May 2002. Published by Zimbel Press in United in *Love: New Solos for Weddings*, 2004.

VOCAL WORKS (Art Songs):

Miscellaneous Songs for Soprano, 1948. Written at Yale University.

Four Songs for Soprano, 1948. Written at Yale University. Texts by Dorothy Diemer Hendry.

"Psalm 137 for Voice and Piano," 1950. Written at Yale School of Music. Premiered at Yale in 1950.

A Miscellany of Love Songs, 1972-73. Texts by American and English poets. Written for Harlan Snow at Santa Barbara, CA. Premiered by him at Northwestern University, 1973.

Seven Somewhat Silly Songs, 1996. Texts by Ogden Nash, Dorothy Parker, Emily Dickinson, Edward Lear. Premiered by Audrey Sharpe, soprano, and ELD, piano, at Santa Barbara Music Club, February, 1997.

Now, while you mull over that and have a sip of tea or coffee or just escape, I'll go on to some of the choral music in other stories and wonderful text sources. Be prepared....

Writing Easy Piano Pieces

Did you ever play "The Happy Farmer" as a child learning to play the piano? I certainly did, and I remember it all these years later (ninety or so).

I sat down and played it this morning, and then of course went off on a lot of variations — different keys, moods, chords, rhythms. The poor farmer was lost after awhile. Lost in the fields, in the crops. F-major gone, gone...but that's not the point of this article (composers are crazy).

The melody was in the *left hand!!!!* Good! It was in the middle of the keyboard — *ho hum!* It was tuneful, memorable! *Wonderful!*

Robert Schumann (he and Clara) had several children. I wonder if they played "The Happy Farmer" from *Album for the Young*. I'm not a Schumann scholar, per se, so I don't know.

But I do know a lot about Robert Schumann's music. *He was able to write difficult music* and also *easy music* and make it *attractive.*

When I was starting to compose and developing a technique on the piano, I wrote some little pieces as a child, and two piano concertos in my teens — lost works — and went on to write difficult piano music at Eastman, at Yale. Nothing much came of these interesting, I thought, but difficult works.

After I graduated from music school, I spent a few months teaching piano to children and wrote some "children's pieces". I thought *"Aha!"* maybe this is the way to be known as a piano composer! But I had no luck interesting a publisher at that time.

(Years later, Isolde Weiermueller-Backes and her husband, Dieter, did publish some of those pieces in their music publishing company, Certosa Verlag, in Germany. *Suite No. 1 for Children. Four on a Row.* They specialize in music by women.)

So when, after some years, I had luck having choral music published, I compensated by not only having a piano part but by making it interesting for the pianist. (*The Three Madrigals* is an example.)

I read through a lot of easy piano music written for children and was amazed at the lack of imagination in the writing: usually in C major, middle register, 4/4 time. *And vowed to write something different.*

Some of the "great" composers *have* written music that is considered easy: Schumann, Bartok especially (*Microcosmos*), Beethoven, Stravinsky even!, Kabalevsky, Hindemith. And many other composers. Jazz composers of course. (Ragtime. I don't consider ragtime easy, unless it is memorized.)

One does not "stoop" to writing easy music. One "rises to it", if possible. In other words, it is *hard* to write easy music that is interesting. And by interesting I mean not necessarily in C major and in the middle register and in 4/4 time.

In later years, along with two more piano concertos, I did have luck having several easier collections published, and Helen Marlais, editor at FJH Music Company, asked me to write more contemporary piano music that was not impossibly difficult. I did, and she chose covers of abstract art for her publications, and I could use, in the pieces, things like:

- extreme registers
- tone clusters
- irregular meters

- atonality
- modality
- pedal techniques (most pianos have *three* pedals)
- repeated patterns
- polychords
- playing on the strings — dampening, *glissandos*, tapping, etc.
- even playing a rhythm on the music rack

You can imagine that many piano teachers rise up in horror, do not take to those sorts of musical elements, those sounds on the piano. But some do — the late Avonell Jackson of Santa Barbara was one. And others. And some children.

My idea was that if children, young people, even adults become accustomed to something besides C major and middle register and 4/4 time, they will like contemporary music better.

And *titles*. One must have evocative, descriptive titles. So on the birthday concert that I mentioned in another story, I played and talked a bit about "In a Dark Cave" and "In a High Steeple" and "Sailing on a Quiet Sea" and others that composers have inspired themselves with, thinking about, expressing something in music.

So the wonderful *piano* must have music written for it not only in C major and middle register and 4/4 time....

Violinist and Teacher Philip Ficsor with whom Emma Lou collaborated often on music for his recitals and students

Two People I wrote a Lot of Music for

O r should that be "two people for whom I wrote a lot of music". Marilyn or my sister — both of them English teachers — would correct me. This is career stuff for my record, so you're welcome to tune out. But Happy Fourth of July, wear your masks, and keep a social distance! We all, young and old, need to get through this!

I've already mentioned some individuals, actual people, for whom I've written an instrumental work or two, usually because they asked me, and they included Mark Thomas (a flute concerto), Betty Oberacker (a piano concerto), John Russo (*Poem of Remembrance for Clarinet and Chamber Orchestra*), Frank Meredith (a euphonium piece), Tachell Gerbert and Bradley Gregory (*The Sea*, and others), Nozomi Takahashi ("Toccata for Piano"), Barbara Harbach ("Toccata for Harpsichord"), Karen Knecht ("Fantasy for Piano"), Amanda Wilson ("Toccata for Amanda"), Isolde Weiermüller-Backes (piano, organ, piano/flute/trumpet pieces), Ronald Horner ("Toccata for Timpani"), John and Teresa Harbaugh (brass works), Dan and Amy Cherry (brass works), Margo Halsted ("Fantasy for Carillon", "Golden Sounds"), other carillon pieces for Ennis Fruhauf, James Welch, June Catchpoole (in Australia), Wesley Arai ("Golden Sounds"), for Stanley Huffman & Eddy Kronengold ("Before Spring for Violin and Piano"), Carol Lancaster (*Sonata No. 3*), vocal works for Audrey Sharpe (*Seven Somewhat Silly Songs*), Janice Veca (sacred songs), Millie and Tod Fortner (sacred songs),

Robert Wilke (sacred song), Mary Silver (sacred song), and for Ellen Grolman and Joan Dixon (*Improvisations for Cello and Piano*), pieces/works written for organists Julie Neufeld, Josephine Brummel, David Gell, Nelson Huber, Mahlon Balderston, Carson Cooman, Marilyn Mason (*Variations on Endless Song*), Martha Chapman (*I Danced in the Morning*), Wyatt Smith, Elena Kalashnikova and Luca Massaglia ("Covfefe"), Thomas Joyce, William Haller, and others including the Santa Barbara Symphony (*Homage to Tchaikovsky, Chumash Dance Celebration, Santa Barbara Overture*, piano concerto). And there were so many choral directors for whom I've written music: Jennifer Morgan Flory of Georgia State College and Jennifer Tibbens and Ginger Colla and Nathan Kreitzer and Rebecca Scott and Patricia Hacker and Carl Zytowski and Conan Castle and Matthew Carey and Daniel Gee and many others.

But there are two individuals, musicians, for whom I wrote an inordinate amount of music, relatively speaking. They are the violinist Philip Ficsor and the organist Joan DeVee Dixon. I'll write something about each of them only in relation to the music, and will leave it up to the reader to learn biographical and personal details about these persons. As far as I know, they are not acquainted, but their motivations regarding me are purely and wonderfully involved only with music and the writing of it. But during the course of music writing and the performing of it they both became dear friends of mine.

One day in 1998 I received a letter from Joan DeVee Dixon, whom I did not know. She had come across my organ collection *Psalms for Organ* and wrote that she wanted either me or another composer to work on a commissioning project she and her husband-to-be, Alvin Broyles, had in mind: to set all of the psalms to music. I, of course, wrote back that I would like to pursue that project. Fortunately, the other composer declined because of previous obligations.

So Joan, a woman forty or so years younger than myself, and I embarked on this venture. I did meet her

Organist Joan DeVee Dixon and Emma Lou enjoying the beauty of the California countryside c 1998

in due time, on a trip she made to Santa Barbara. Over the course of a few years I wrote over 50 different pieces for her. She chose the psalms that she wanted interpreted musically and the medium. Some of the works were for solo organ — two collections of "seasonal psalms" and several "psalm interpretations"— and there were groups of individual pieces for flute and organ, trumpet and organ, bass trombone and organ, percussion and organ, and one larger work on Psalm 121 for organ, brass, and percussion.

She arranged for the recording of all this music in the chapel of the university with which her fiancé was associated, and she got together the various musicians, all excellent, to record all of the music. I came for the recordings and did a little playing but Joan herself recorded almost all of the organ parts.

I took delight in writing so much music, and I believe it was easy for several reasons: 1) the psalms themselves are beautiful and evocative and often visual, 2) the different mediums provided a wide variety of expression and style, 3) I have always been a prolific composer and need only a word or two or a phrase to start the imagination working musically. For instance, "I lift my eyes to the hills…" or "my tears have been my food by day and by night" or "why do the nations rage, and the peoples plot in vain?" or "the Lord is my rock, and my fortress, and my deliverer". Most composers are sensitive to words and meanings; I certainly am.

Joan was eager to finish the project (her fiancé, whom she had married during this period, was not in good health, and he had provided the funds and much of the instigation), and ultimately, I set most of the psalms in some medium or another. I had already used many of them in choral and solo works, but some of them more than once, so the total number of settings was larger than the number of psalms. But I used more than 75 percent of the book of 150 psalms and at Joan's request even Psalm 151, one of those discovered in the Dead Sea Scrolls. My setting for organ of this psalm is one of the more difficult pieces.

Most of the settings, though not easy, are not extremely difficult to perform and are in traditional notation rather than any kind of innovative, graphic form.

All of this music was published and available from one publisher or another.

Emma Lou composed more than 50 pieces for organ for Joan DeVee Dixon, most centered around the Psalms of the Bible

So I am grateful to Joan, an active church music director, composer/arranger, former university professor, and a fine organist, for a productive period of music writing, and for her friendship.

The other person who came into my musical life, a bit later than Joan, was (is) Philip Ficsor, a musician also about 40 years younger than I. I first met him in 2008 when he visited the church where I was organist — First Presbyterian in Santa Barbara. The organist there at the time, Nelson Huber, had mentioned Phil to me so I knew that he was on the music faculty at Westmont College and a superlative violinist. Phil knew of my organ music from his previous church connections, I believe. I don't remember the exact moment he asked me to write something for him but probably at a little lunch get-together at El Encanto with Nelson and myself.

The "something" turned out to be, at Phil's request, his wish to record all of my violin music and for me to write more works for him. I had written a violin sonata while a student at Yale, and in 1988 the virtuosic "Catch-A-Turian Toccata" (for a duo who didn't like it much, but is one of my more interesting and difficult works).

Marilyn and Emma Lou often spent enjoyable days with Phil Ficsor at their home in Santa Barbara where Phil and Emma worked on music

The first work I wrote for Phil was a suite *Summer Day* that had three movements: "Summer Day", "Elegy", "Jazz Romp", and dates from 2008. We performed it at SB Music Club and then at First Presbyterian at a concert of all the works, and most recently at a concert of my music for my 90th birthday for Music Club at Trinity Episcopal. It is a happy work — well, the "Elegy" is more introspective, freer, not rhythmic-based like the outer movements.

Phil wanted some more music written for him, so in 2012, I wrote a concerto that he played with the Westmont

College orchestra conducted by Michael Shasberger. The movements evolved first from a piece Phil asked me to write, in a romantic style, resulting in "Remembrance of Things Past" and I added "A Little Parlour Music—After Poulenc", "Santa Barbara Rag", and "John Adams Light".

And he wanted some hymn arrangements and I wrote three for him. However, he found the "Amazing Grace" arrangement too plain, so I wrote another with a little more zip.

Also I arranged, with just a little register change, "Homage to Paderewski", originally for viola, and we added that to his repertoire.

Before Phil and his family moved to Colorado in 2013, I wrote a parting piece, "Going Away", that was quite programmatic, with his family packing up and saying goodbye and departing.

We recorded all these works, with TrueTone Productions' Dan Bos set up in my living room and Phil standing near a window in a far corner where I could see him, but separated by an array of microphones. We spent several mornings recording, broken at intervals by brownies consumption. It was one of the pleasantest times a composer could have. Then Phil and Dan edited the many takes of all the pieces while I mostly looked on. They could edit down to the smallest increment of pitch or beat.

(I had rather recently had a mild heart attack, and if I balked a little at yet another take on a passage or piece during the recording sessions, Phil had us forge on.)

It's all on *YouTube* if anyone cares to listen.

Phil is a consummate musician and teacher. He was meticulous in asking what I, the composer, intended. He had numerous suggestions for bowing and occasionally the use of double stops.

Why he chose to spend so much of his time learning a fairly minor composer's music, I don't know. He had recorded the violin music of William Bolcom, now mine. Not a bad recommendation, from my viewpoint.

TOCCATA FOR PIANO

for Nozomi Takahashi

EMMA LOU DIEMER

Toccata for Piano and Nozomi Takahashi

I'm not sure why there is this compulsion to write things down but guess it has something to do with wanting to "create" — something, so you'll have to bear with me. This is about a former student and a musical work.

At UCSB I had in one of my theory classes a Japanese student named Nozomi Takahashi. She was a small, vibrant young woman — smart (she had perfect pitch) and funny and she brightened up the class atmosphere as so many students do.

Sometimes, very seldom, she would have "black outs" and suddenly freeze, not move, seem to be in another world. It must have been some kind of imbalance in her diet — I never found out. She didn't have a seizure, just a freeze-in-place moment.

One day in 1979, before her final year, she asked me to write a piano piece for her senior graduation recital. Nozomi was a piano student of Betty Oberacker, for whom I have written a piano concerto and a concert piece, "Encore".

I had been "working in" the electronic medium for a few years, finding some new ways to create timbre, but being turned off by the prepared piano works in which keys were marked off with tape — although I did a little of that — and objects inserted between the strings and the plink here, the plunk there, the disconnected, melody-less, irreverent writing for the piano. It was the "here" and "there" that disturbed me the most. For musical ideas I like to have direction and a continuation of the sound part of the time and homages to rhythm and suggestions of tonality and my interpretation of meaning (rather than a collection of effects).

So in the writing of a toccata for Nozomi I wrote a piece that used both dampening of the strings and sometimes playing *glissandos* on the strings and even striking them — not too hard — and not neglecting any register of the piano, and transitioning gradually between playing on the keyboard and making those sounds on the strings.

I'm sure Nozomi had never played anything like that piece and she had to lean over and reach the strings while keeping the pedal down in some places. But she played it beautifully in her recital. She told me afterward that she had a momentary "black out" at one point, but it wasn't noticeable to me or anyone.

I corresponded with her for a few years after she returned to Japan, and she later wrote that she was proud of her little boy who was good in art, but I have lost track of her, sadly.

But there is a history to the toccata I wrote for her. One day Clara Lyle Boone was passing through Santa Barbara and phoned me to ask if I had any music I could send her. Clara had started her own publishing company, specializing in music by women composers. I sent her the toccata and she published it with an abstract art cover as she did all her publications. It somehow won a *Seventeen Magazine* contest and was brought to the attention of some young pianists and their teachers.

In the next few years, in spite of the relative obscurity of the publisher and the fact that the score was a facsimile of the manuscript, had no measure lines, and called for standing and playing on the strings part of the time — in spite of all that, some pianists discovered it and there are several recordings on *YouTube*. Clara had it transcribed into computer notation and it found its way into a collection called *Music Without Borders* with Nozomi's piece entitled "Toccata for Piano".

It's about the only piece of music of mine, in addition to the *Three Madrigals*, that anyone knows anything about.

So, thank you, Nozomi, dear former theory student, wherever you are!

Conductor Nan Washburn who collaborated with Emma Lou on a piece, Suite of Homages, that was played by the Women's Philharmoic in San Francisco in November 1985

The Women's Philharmonic and Music By Women

As I write, we in Santa Barbara have had day after day of gorgeous weather, as though Mother Nature is compensating for confining us in our homes in fear of catching or spreading the virus.

Mother's Day, *Mother* Nature. This article is about women-something, mostly.

In about 1985 Nan Washburn came to see me. Nan graduated from UCSB; she was a flute major, a student of Bernie Atkinson. She was also a founder of the *Women's* Philharmonic in San Francisco and one of its conductors. You can read about Nan; her conducting career has been exemplary for many years, including her tenure as conductor of the Michigan Philharmonic, but many other orchestras.

The Women's Philharmonic performed only music by women and the members of the orchestra were only women and the conductors were only women.

Nan wanted to know if I would write a work for the Women's Philharmonic, which I did (*Suite of Homages*), but that isn't the subject of this article.

The subject is *Women's* anything. Women bristle at being called "woman composer", "woman doctor", etc. (that designation was never necessary for men — how often in history books did you read of "man doctor", "man composer"?).

Ok, so you women want to be known as just "composer". Granted. But it wasn't always so. (By the way, our country has never been able to elect a *Woman* president; there must be something wrong — and it isn't men who are preventing this, it is probably women).

The *Women's* movement seemed to be really stirring in the 1970s. And for *Women* composers there began to be festivals of *Women's* music. I organized one at UCSB (it wasn't one of the major ones but an early one).

Composers who came and gave presentations included Pauline Oliveros and Nancy Van de Vate and Toshiko Akiyoshi, jazz pianist, who is now 90 years old. (Oliveros died in 2016; she was one of the pioneers in tape music/ electronic music, and had one of her "deep listening" sessions in Storke Plaza where several people lay down in a circle and produced random long tones.)

As an aside, I played programs of organ works by *Women* composers in those days. I didn't know any, so I sent out a search in a women composers' publication. One of the works I played was by Clare Shore ("Outlands Sketches").

Another sidelight: one of the composers who answered the call for scores was a *man* who later became a well-known *man* composer, probably because he had the gumption to send his scores anywhere they might be of interest.

Also, at UCSB, I played a concert of music, mostly for piano, by women composers. I remember that 155 people came. Interesting, the facts one remembers. It received a great review in the paper by Ardis Higgins, local advocate for women's causes and a strong member of the SB Symphony board.

There was the first *Woman* composer to win a Pulitzer Prize; since then there have been several women who have won, but she will always be known as the first.

I've watched women composers' reputations peek a bit and then plunge downward — kind of like the coronavirus curve as it leaves New York.

(Oh, to be a Brahms whose music and name live on forever!)

Our knowledge of what women accomplish is somewhat limited, so we need to study about them. I have a niece who is a doctor, one who is an engineer, one the co-founder of a research company, a personnel director, a program manager, a school principal, a minister. a math teacher, a graphic artist, an organist/pianist/harpist, a poet, a trumpet major, a commercial pilot, etc.

I like to think that people don't say *Woman* doctor, *Woman* engineer, but one can't help but notice that they are women, right?

I've never won a Pulitzer Prize, never will. Nor a Guggenheim (tried twice, but discovered that a fellow composer whom I asked for a recommendation was also applying) — you *see*: women give up too easily. Peggy Granville-Hicks, an Australian composer who died in 1990 applied, I believe it was 17 times, before she finally received a Guggenheim fellowship. Some women don't give up. Or, I could add, do not live in the right place or know the "right people". Sometimes, as in any endeavor, extreme talent is not the road to fame. And much is lost.

We're happy to write, happy there are people who like it, happy to be alive in Santa Barbara on this gorgeous, gorgeous day in May, 2020. Thank you, Mother Nature. Thank you, my mother (and father). Thank you, Mother/Father God.

Ruminations on Composing

Julia Child lived in Santa Barbara during her last years; we caught glimpses of her now and then. One of her quotes was in this morning's paper: "Find something you're passionate about and keep tremendously interested in it." That certainly applies to us who are in the music field, and we composers tend to be especially obsessed.

When I begin to think, in the very early morning hours, of all the music I've written, and the people for whom I've written it, before long the light is bright through the window.

Not counting music written for forces outside of Santa Barbara, but just in Santa Barbara, at the university, I was privileged to write pieces for several faculty artist performers (here go some name-dropping):

Carillonists Ennis Fruhauf, Jim Welch, Margo Halsted, Wesley Arai: pieces for each of them, the last one very recent (played by Wesley last year at the golden anniversary of the UCSB carillon).

Oboist Clayton Wilson and flutist Bernie Atkinson: a piece that included harpsichord and pre-recorded tape. We had fun putting it together.

Carl Zytowski, for his unique high tenor voice: a song cycle and two works for his men's ensemble, The Schubertians.

Geoffrey Rutkowski: a virtuoso cello work (the husband of a friend of mine found it "frightening"; Geoff changed not one note).

Betty Oberacker: a piano concerto and a solo work ("Encore") in which she "burned up the piano" according to the local reviewer. Betty can have a piece memorized in days.

Wendell Nelson and Marjorie (Mrs. Nelson): pieces for two pianos and for piano four hands. Magic when they played together. Some of my best work, if I may say so.

And for Tachell Gerbert and Bradley Gregory, former students of Wendell: two works, one for two pianos, one for piano four hands (just written and awaiting performance after the disappearance of the coronavirus).

For another former student at UCSB, Nozomi Takahashi: "Toccata for Piano." You can hear several recordings of it on *YouTube*.

And in town, earlier, at my church: anthems for the choir and its director, Julie Neufeld; solos for choir members Audry Sharpe, Janice Veca, Mary Silver, Bob Wilkc, Millie and Tod Fortner.

Organ pieces for David Gell, Josephine Brummel, Julie Neufeld, Nelson Huber, Mahlon Balderston. Thomas Joyce.

Four pieces for the Santa Barbara Symphony.

Many violin works for former Santa Barbara resident/ Westmont professor Philip Ficsor.

And for "inanimate" instruments: a suite for the Sabathil harpsichord that the music department once had. It was a two-manual and possessed a 16-foot stop (any note played sounded an octave lower). And a totally serial piece for the Flentrop organ in Lotte Lehmann Concert Hall. (Some passages call for a stop to be gradually engaged). I think only two organists have played this piece, Jim Welch and myself.)

Although all the above are published, they are probably gathering dust in someone's music files or in the publisher archives or a library somewhere. But it is a joy to write music for outstanding musicians.

As for longevity, immortality, think of the Bach *St. Matthew Passion* and his *Mass in B Minor*, both monumental masterpieces and pretty much forgotten until Mendelssohn resurrected them years after they were written.

There is always hope — in resurrection.

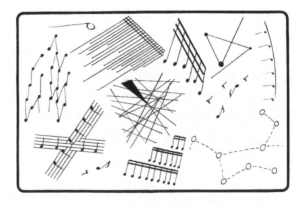

HOMAGE

✎ Cowell, Cage,
        Crumb and Czerny

for TWO PIANOS

By
Emma Lou Diemer

plymouth music co., inc. • 170 n.e. 33rd st. • ft. lauderdale, fl 33334

Homages Schomages

Here's another "me-ness" article/story/essay for what will eventually turn into a kindle series (if I can figure out how to do that). Bulletin! My nephew-in-law, Steve Gierhart, is helping me with that endeavor. He is an excellent publisher, editor, writer, tech person.

Think how interesting it would have been if some of the "great masters" had written about their own works and lives. Of course they were too busy writing their music; but I've written a great amount of music, too, and like the idea of writing about some of it. If not I, who? There have been dissertations, some articles, a few critiques, and here is more information for your reading pleasure or disdain.

This particular essay is about the writing of *Homages*. The origin of "homage" was a public acknowledgement by a man of the greatness of his feudal lord. So this is a public acknowledgement by a woman of the music she has created.

Oh, oh — you've tuned out already. I will proceed, regardless. Who but the composer can best discuss her own music? I ask you.

Three of the "homages" are from the 1980s while I was on the UCSB faculty, a period of more imagination, inspiration?

"Homage to Cowell, Cage, Crumb, and Czerny" for two pianos was written in 1981 for Wendell and Marjorie Nelson (Wendell was chair of the UCSB piano faculty). The piece was published by Colla Voce.

It is an eclectic work, and I think an entertaining one, and pays homage to the composers in the title in the following ways: Henry Cowell for the "aeolian harp" device of holding down certain keys and strumming with the other hand the corresponding strings. (No pedal for this kind of effect.) The John Cage influence is reflected in the number of times a pattern is played (Cage was a devotee of numerology among other things. I heard him perform in Washington, D.C. once, his work with a number of radios tuned to different stations and manipulated, changed at random). There is no "chance", however, in my piece. George Crumb for clusters, string dampening, string *glissandos*, light finger movement on the strings, pedal techniques. Czerny for repeated patterns that furnish the intimations of tonality.

I remember hearing the Nelsons perform this work in Lotte Lehmann Concert Hall at UCSB and watching from the corner of my eye the students in the audience who were there for credit for a class and had not the slightest idea what the music was about. They occasionally tittered. I thought the piece, the work, was quite effective and elicited the proverbial tears in my eyes when it finished. (Tears in the eyes of the composer mean the work held together, created an impression, was what one had expected and hoped for.)

I tried to interest a piano team who professed encouragement for new works — tried to interest them in the composition, to no avail. I guess one must have a Pulitzer or some magic elixir to get performers' attention? Or be good friends with the composer, as were the Nelsons.

In 1985 I composed *Suite of Homages* for the Women's Philharmonic in San Francisco, and the premiere was conducted by JoAnn Falletta. It is probably my best orchestral work. The homages are to Poulenc, Stravinsky, Webern, Ligeti, and Prokofiev.

The Poulenc movement is effervescent, tonal, joyful, rhythmic.

The Stravinsky is largely tonal and uses *ostinatos*, layered melodic patterns, shifting accents, an abrupt ending (no romance there).

The Webern is atonal, serial, goes to the middle and then strictly retrogrades (instruments, pitches and all), is quite transparent and objective.

The Ligeti has dramatic clusters of repeated chords in the different choirs of the orchestra. It is non-metric, and has no melodic ideas whatsoever.

The Prokofiev is a wash of exuberance and virtuosic fragments and flourishes especially in the woodwinds. (Nan Washburn, first flutist, who had approached me about writing this work requested a showy flute part.)

I remember that Joan Tower, who also had a work on the concert, said with some surprise that she was "impressed".

In an earlier essay/story I stated that when I heard for the first time an orchestra piece of mine, it sounded foreign. Not so with *Suite of Homages* — they sounded exactly as I had imagined. That is progress. The work is published by Seesaw.

In 1987 I wrote another work for Wendell and Marjorie Nelson, a piece that is more emotional and even more structural, pianistic, and virtuosic than the earlier "homage". It is "Variations for Piano Four Hands — Homage to Ravel, Schoenberg, and May Aufderheide".

The whole work is based on a 12-chord series, and the chords are quite lush and impressionistic. In each variation they are treated differently — sometimes in a "Daphnis and Chloe" kind of textural richness, sometimes contrapuntally, using the lowest note of each chord as a tone row. The ragtime rhythm of May Aufderheide is suggested in one variation in a leisurely fashion. All the playing is on the keyboard except in a transition back to the beginning, using string dampening for a few measures in single notes.

I remember testing the opening of the work by having my friend Marilyn "play around" with the first chord sonority while I added the treble part. (It is hard for one person to play 4-hand piano music.) Bradley Gregory and Tachell Gerbert have played this work; I wish more pianists would. Colla Voce publishes it and the Nelsons recorded it on CRS.

In 1997 Martha MacDonald in Austin, Texas presented a concert of my music and asked me to write a viola/piano piece for a then-local violist, Kathryn Steely, which I did, and titled it "Homage to Paderewski". Many of us learned Paderewski's "Minuet in G" as children, and while I was writing the new piece that minuet came to mind and soon worked its way into the music in a fanciful way, lending life to a middle section. The rest of the work is more expressive and thoughtful. I later made a version for violin and Philip Ficsor and I performed and recorded it. Seesaw published the original version.

Homage to Poulenc, Mozart, and MacDowell for flute, cello, and piano was written in 2004 for flutist Michael Finegold and the Essex Chamber Players. They recorded it and it is published by Kaiser/Southern. The Poulenc connection again is the melodic, enticing and rather humorous element. Mozart is almost directly quoted in some places in the first and last movements, and the basis of the middle movement is MacDowell's "To a Wild Rose", a brief piano piece that Mrs. (Marian) MacDowell rescued from the waste basket where Edward had tossed it. Most of us played that piece in the early days of piano study. I use its principal motive through most of the movement and its character is plaintive, nostalgic.

Lastly, one of the commissions I've received from the AGO (American Guild of Organists) was for the 2016 convention in Houston. I didn't feel like writing a big, ho-hum, *au courant* organ piece and instead wrote a rather mischievous one, "Homage to Bach and Widor". It's a bit of a parody on the composers' two works that are the best-known of all organ literature: Johann Sebastian Bach's *Toccata and Fugue in D Minor* and the "Toccata" from Charles-Marie Widor's *Symphony for Organ, no. 5*.

I use very familiar motives from both works in a free fantasy style. Diane Meredith Belcher was to have performed it at the convention, but she fell ill and Canadian organist Ken Cowan learned it in a few days and played it, memorized, in Houston. (I wish someone would publish it — it's a fun piece, a bit of a "spoof". So boring to be a long-hair, solemn organ composer all the time....)

So much for *Homages* for now....

SECTION FOUR
Performing and Recording

The modern facade of San Francisco's Cathedral of St. Mary's of the Assumption

Recital at Saint Mary's in San Francisco

One weekend, in San Francisco, some years ago, thanks to David Hatt, I gave an organ recital at the Cathedral of St. Mary's of the Assumption, that gorgeous edifice at 1111 Gough Street. (Notice the "elevens" in the address). There is no structure like it, inside or out.

I happened to play there because I met Dave, one of the Cathedral organists, at an American Guild of Organists (AGO) convention and he invited me. Incidentally, I've found that even if you're not a world-famous organist, but have a little tiny bit of recognition, you can ask to play at various venues. That is how I came to give recitals (of mostly my own music) at the Cathedral of Our Lady of the Angels in Los Angeles, another "drop dead" gorgeous "church" and Grace Cathedral in San Francisco and even Washington National Cathedral. (I should have asked to play at some others like St. Patrick's in NYC or Riverside or Notre Dame or any number of out-of-this-world places, but one runs out of time — and one can't live one's life all over again, or really want to, I think. But it would have been fun.)

Anyway, the first time I walked into St. Mary's I was blown away (literally, in windy San Francisco) by the interior, the diaphanous "chandelier", the space, the art work in the alcoves, the Ruffatti organ — so it was a delight to have a chance to play there. There weren't many at the recital (kind of hard to fill up 2400 seats with a pretty much unknown

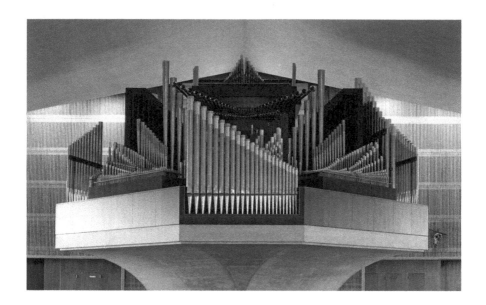

The pipes of the Ruffatti at Cathedral of St. Mary's of the Assumption seen in closeup and through the Nave

recitalist not playing Bach or Widor, etc.), but that's not the main reason for writing about this experience. (And I did play there a couple of more times, always a pleasure.)

It is that after practicing late the last evening before the recital, Marilyn and I left — on that wildly windy Saturday night — to find a taxi to return to our hotel. We came out of the Cathedral and crossed the busy intersections and stood on a corner, looking forlorn, I imagine, abandoned, anxious, wind-blown, two women in need of help.

The cars whizzed by (they always "whiz") and did I mention the wind? And we were not a little cold and there was no help in sight.

Suddenly a taxi, a block or more away and several lanes over, darted through traffic and over the lanes, horns honking at it, and arrived miraculously in front of us. The driver was Middle Eastern, Iranian, Egyptian, Israeli, who knows? We never found out. He spoke no English. He gathered us up, rescued us in spite of danger to himself and his car, and deposited us at our hotel safely.

I remember that more than the Cathedral, the organ recital, the city. I remember the kindness of an intrepid taxi driver, one of the "foreigners" in our dear country.

The exterior view of Rome's only Medieval Gothic church, the Santa Maria sopra Minerva

Recital in Rome

On July 4, 2000, I played an organ recital at Santa Maria sopra Minerva in Rome, Italy. It wasn't an auspicious event. There weren't many people in attendance. The tourists roaming the church were there to see Michelangelo's *Risen Christ* marble sculpture to the left of the main altar. And to view the Gothic interior (a contrast to the Renaissance style facade). The church dates from the 13th century. It is Rome's only Medieval Gothic church.

It was built over the ruins of a temple dedicated to the Egyptian goddess Isis (mistakenly ascribed to the Greco-Roman goddess Minerva). It is a block from the Pantheon.

But I'm not here to write about architecture or sculpture — about which I know very little — but about the recital, and the aftermath.

I was asked to give the recital, which consisted of music by women composers, by Patricia Adkins Chiti, president and founder of Fondazione Adkins Chiti: Donne in Musica. I did not know Patricia Chiti, but Suzanne Summerville of the University of Alaska-Fairbanks had suggested my name to her. (Women have these little networks, too!). Patricia arranged the beautiful venue.

You can read about Patricia Chiti in many reference sources: she was British, an extremely active proponent of women in music, a singer and musicologist and author, married to Italian composer Gian Paolo Chiti. She died unexpectedly in 2018.

I met her briefly before the recital — one could not miss her abundant head of beautiful red hair. She arranged so many concerts, attended so many conferences and festivals for years, that I doubt she lingered afterward.

The organ, pipe of course, old, was high up in a gallery that overlooked the nave of the church. The console could not be seen from "down below", but through the grill I could look down on the people and the group of chairs where the listeners sat.

I had climbed several sets of stairs, passed through several rooms (Dressing rooms? Rehearsal rooms?) to get to the organ. And I sat at the console directly under the blower and mechanical actions. It was quite hot, and I had no idea what the sound of the organ would be down in the nave. About all I could hear was the blower and the mechanism of the workings of the organ.

But I played the program — pieces by Marilyn Ziffrin, Theophane Hytrek, Harrier Boltz, Clare Shore, Violet Archer, Clara Schumann, Fanny Mendelssohn, Diemer — and heard a scattering of applause coming from the marble space far down. I turned off the organ, gathered the music up, probably changed my shoes, and began the descent through the many rooms and down the many steps and into the area where the listeners had been. There was no one there. (It had taken me too long to descend, I guess, and the people had returned to, melted into the glories of Rome and its churches. A faithful friend or two were waiting of course.)

But I will always remember it — the heat up under the clacking of the organ, the fact that it was our Independence Day, a chance to play in Rome, the disappearing audience music!

The pipes beautiful pipes for the organ at the Santa Maria sopra Minerva where Emma Lou played in 2000

Abbey Roads Studios in London, studio of the Beatles, where Emma Lou's *Santa Barbara Overture* **was recorded with the London Symphony and conductor Brynmor Llewelyn Jones in 1991**

Recording in London, Prague, and Bratislava

At some point in one's life as a composer — who has written a rather large work, in fact several, that one believes should be "out there" — one thinks about having those works recorded "for all posterity".

One is well aware of the 1,000th recording of a Mozart symphony, the 500th of a concerto by Beethoven, the millions of recordings in the pop category (songs/videos that spike and disappear or become pop classics). And one thinks "why not mine?".

If not being begged by Deutshe Grammophon to record one's music, there are alternatives if one has the wherewithal, the finances to have that happen. Amy Beach — who came from a well-off family and married a "well-off" doctor — would have had the resources. Or if one applies to one of the funds set up by a successful composer to help other composers; or if one has "skimped and saved" money from whatever profession one had followed in addition to composing. If one of those solutions is available, one looks forward to having two or three of one's works recorded professionally.

There is this urge to have some works that a composer considers among the best he or she has produced, to let it have a wider audience before the coffin closes over its head, so to speak.

I was one of a number of composers who were phoned by two of the entrepreneurs — composers themselves — who have contacts with orchestras all over the world, but especially in Eastern Europe, and could arrange for contemporary works to be recorded by one or more of those orchestras.

I had "skimped and saved" and said yes to William Thomas McKinley of MMC Recordings for the recording of my *Santa Barbara Overture* and the 1991 piano concerto and yes to Joel Suben of "Save the Music" for the recording, with some help from the publisher, of my marimba concerto.

(I have had other works recorded, without my help, by excellent musicians, including Marilyn Mason and my organ concerto, *Alaska*, but this is about three particular works, and there is a certain amount of adventure.)

In the case of MMC I could choose the orchestra, and thought the London Symphony — well, yes — would be a good one. I stress that the London Symphony did not approach me (*That* would be The Day). The piece was *Santa Barbara Overture*.

So one fair morning — I think it was 1991 — my friend Marilyn (I keep mentioning her, and have written about this amazing person previously) and I set out for London, and I remember us getting off the plane, finding a taxi, and dragging our roll-away suitcases to the Abbey Road Studios at 3 Abbey Road, St John's Wood, City of Westminster, London. *Wikipedia* tells us "It was established in November 1931 by the Gramophone Company, a predecessor of British music company EMI, which owned it until Universal Music took control of part of EMI in 2013".

It was also the studio where the Beatles experimented and recorded many of their albums.

We were escorted up to the recording booth, overlooking, through a glass, the entire London Symphony assembled in a huge room down below. The conductor, Brynmor Llewelyn Jones, came in to discuss the score to *Santa Barbara Overture* a little, and then they began to rehearse and record.

They had some trouble with the opening, which changes meter and accent often — they had to play it over a few times. When it settled down to a more regular beat, all was fine.

Composer and Conductor Brynmor Llewelyn Jones conducting 1980s

It was quite something to hear one's music played by a very large, major orchestra. (Kind of like hearing the Mormon Tabernacle singing a simple choral piece?). I didn't have any interaction with the musicians except perhaps with the pianist afterward who liked his part.

The conductor seemed pleased. So much for another American composer's music dispatched by an out-of-this-world symphony orchestra. The work was ultimately released on an album with the other compositions written about in this article — put out there "for posterity" to hear.

The recording session lasted only a few hours and then we were off to be in London — the Victoria and Albert Museum where, at the cafeteria, Marilyn knocked down a big pile of dishes from above the buffet and I lost control of my tray and dumped the contents on the floor. (Someone asked if we were Americans. We sneaked out without eating and avoided that area for the rest of our tour)

I remember that we stayed in Kensington and that the hair dryer adapter was wrong. Little tidbits of experience that everyone has on trips.

In 1995, we went with Betty Oberacker to Prague to record my piano concerto that was written for her. The orchestra was the Czech Radio Symphony Orchestra conducted by Vladimir Válek. I remember quite well meeting the conductor in the recording studio before recording and him saying to me "this piece is quite impossible". Someone said he tells that to all the composers, but it wasn't much comfort. However, he did a creditable job and said afterward that he liked the concerto.

Slovak Radio Building in Braatislava, Czech Republic, where in 2002 Emma Lou's Marimba Concerto was recorded

Betty was disappointed that she could not push him to a faster tempo especially at the beginning. Fright, on his part, I suppose. He had her record the cadenza separately, having dismissed the orchestra after they recorded their part with her in the rest of the concerto.

I think we enjoyed Prague, one of the world's most beautiful cities, more than the recording. The concerto was also performed in an ornate concert hall in a private residence.

We helped Betty carry some famous glassware (crystal?) on the plane going home.

The recording of my marimba concerto took place in 2002 in Bratislava, the capital of the Czech Republic. The orchestra was the Slovak Radio Symphony and the conductor was Joel Eric Suben, whose "Save the Music" project resulted in a number of recordings of American and European music.

This was a pleasant experience all around. Nathan Daughtrey, the marimbist, met me and Marilyn and Marilyn's sister, Sharon, in Vienna, and we drove in a small Mercedes jeep-like car to Bratislava, 45 minutes away and on the Danube River. The entire walk from our hotel to the Radio and Television building, where the recording took place was lined with linden trees. The Bratislava Castle, which we toured, was nearby. Prices were unbelievably low.

Nathan and Joel, both superlative musicians, made a fine recording of the concerto. Nathan is now head of C. Alan Publications, founded by Cort McClaren, and Joel is a prolific composer and conductor.

Incidentally, the marimbist for whom the concerto was written, Deborah Schwartz, has disappeared from my knowledge. Sometimes people do that, haven't you found? (Another disappearance is of Joan Allen Smith, who was a theory teacher at UCSB when I was there. Where are these people? Life's mysteries!....)

The Chapel at the Samarkand in Santa Barbara, one of the last places that Emma Lou played regularly

The Last Places I Played

At the end of the movie *Places in the Heart*, an imaginary scene takes place with the living and the deceased gathered together in church passing Communion from one to another. It is a scene of reconciliation and peace after strife-torn episodes that divided the town. It is a strong film and that last scene remains in one's mind.

The last place I played for services was at Samarkand, in the small chapel in the retirement community that is about five minutes from my house.

The organ in the chapel is from the same company, Johannus, that installed the organ in the chapel at First Presbyterian. The one at First Presbyterian is a little larger, but the one at Samarkand has a *Zimbelstern* (cymbal-star), a stop on the organ that emits a constant tinkling sound. With some organs it is placed near the console and set in motion electrically. On a digital organ it is a sampled zimbelstern sound, a stop on the organ. It is a joyful addition to some of the music.

The Chaplain at Samarkand for most of the last Sundays I played there was Sherry Peterson. Sherry was enjoyable to talk with and listen to in her brief sermons. She also is an expert photographer. I have very close relatives who are ministers and have an avid interest in baseball games. And I find it interesting (revealing?) that people who are intensely involved in religious ministry have a secular, worldly vocation/hobby on the side. A needed balance probably?

At Samarkand there were three or four organists who rotated Sunday playing and two of them were long-time friends, Bill Beasley and Mahlon Balderston. Sadly, they are both fairly recently deceased.

A couple of years ago the SB Music Club honored me on a "*Big O*" birthday with a concert of my own music presented at Trinity Episcopal.

Philip Ficsor came from Colorado to play some of the music with me that I had written for him when he was teaching at Westmont College — a *Suite for Violin and Piano "Summer Day"* and an "Aria". Phil is one of those world-class musicians who has a piece memorized practically minutes after you give it to him, and who finds something in it that you didn't know was there.

Also, Tachell Gerbert and Bradley Gregory drove up from Thousand Oaks and performed my "Variations for Piano Four Hands — Homage to Ravel, Schoenberg, and May Aufderheide", a major piece based on a series of 12 impressionistic, multi-note chords. Some of the variations are colorfully atmospheric; some take the bottom notes of each chord and treat them as a tone row — in one variation a rapid "toccata" in double octaves; another variation has ragtime rhythm in a rather leisurely style (May Aufderheide was a well-known ragtime composer at the turn of the last century; she spent her last years in California). In playing the Variations, Brad and Tachell filled Trinity with resounding pianistic sonorities.

Also on the concert I played three organ pieces: One, "Toccata for a Joyful Day", was written for a wedding at First Presbyterian. "Fiesta" was written to celebrate the Spanish Days Fiesta that takes place every summer in Santa Barbara and has a long, enormous parade up State Street from the wharf. Thousands of spectators watch and hear Spanish and Mexican dancers and bands and there are hundreds of horses — 600 at least.

And I played my setting of "Morning Has Broken" (there is a very popular version of the song sung by Cat

Stevens on *YouTube*). The words are by English poet
Eleanor Farjeon, and the tune is Scottish Gaelic.

> *Morning has broken like the first morning*
> *Blackbird has spoken like the first bird*
> *Praise for the singing*
> *Praise for the morning*
> *Praise for them springing fresh from the Word....*

(It is a nice song to improvise at the piano, in view of
the mountains or hills or anything beautiful, on an early
morning.)

Also on the birthday concert I played a group of short,
descriptive pieces on the piano, and will discuss them later,
after you recover from the above.

Bill Beasley was at the concert, an hour ahead of time,
and so was Mahlon Balderston. Places in the heart.

SECTION FIVE
Churches and I

The Washington Cathedral where Emma Lou played on occasion

Practicing the Organ at Washington National Cathedral

As the world turns — or "as the stomach turns" as Carol Burnett titled one of her soap opera skits — it lurches and tries to right itself. I'll tell one more little story, and then shut up for awhile.

When I moved to the Washington, D.C. area in 1959, the building that I loved most was the Washington National Cathedral (years before I had a similar love-at-first-sight experience when viewing, as a child, Riverside Church in NYC. If you have ever loved a building, you'll know what I mean).

Washington Cathedral, in 1959, was not completed yet but its majestic structure and its oh-so-live acoustics were enough to excite all the gods to worship it.

And the pipe organ! One of my desires was to play the great (and swell and positive and choir and pedal divisions) of that powerful instrument. (Actually, later I did on two or three separate occasions, and gave a recital there some years ago.)

But, returning to 1959, our church choir was to take part in a concert at the cathedral one Sunday and a small portative organ was to be used, not the *big* pipe organ, and I was to play the small, portative organ.

I arrived to practice one evening and was let in from a door somewhere below the nave and escorted up a flight of steps to the huge interior of the cathedral. My escort, a guard actually, *assumed I was to practice on the big organ up in the chancel*, and led me up to it.

I said not a word, and smiled toward the small portative organ as we passed it. You may not think it was a big deal to have a chance to play a world-famous instrument, but it was, for me.

I had, at that juncture, never played an organ in a space in which the sound echoed for more than perhaps two seconds at the most. So I improvised for about an hour and marveled at what one can produce on an extraordinary pipe organ. (That is a whole other subject having to do with what a composer creates on what kind of instrument — what sort of music, what style. Something to ponder and I have, many times. Think about Bach's *Toccata and Fugue in D Minor*, probably the most famous piece in organ literature — the opening of the toccata in a *dead* room as opposed to a very *live* room.).

Anyway, after a while I went down to the waiting portative organ and practiced what I was supposed to.

The Washington Cathedral main organ, the focus of this story

Emma Lou sitting on the organ of First Presbyterian Church in Santa Barbara where she was the organist for 16 years

First Presbyterian
and Church Organ Jobs

This is about a church in town, another "institution" in Santa Barbara that many of us know about and are proud of: First Presbyterian. And its pipe organ.

By way of introduction to this topic, having to do with playing in church, before First Presbyterian in Santa Barbara I was organist in that city at Church of Christ, Scientist — also known as Christian Science. I wasn't a member, but did spend 12 years as organist at the church on Valerio. (Incidentally, that was the only church in my long history that had an "organist's room" complete with a washroom, and chairs to sit in; in all the other churches I floated around in the choir room or back in the sacristy before services. So thank you, Mary Baker Eddy.)

It was a restful period, at the CS church, and I enjoyed especially the Wednesday night "testimonials" when various people stood up and talked about their experiences of being healed through Christian Science. My mother, though not a Christian Scientist, believed in many of the teachings and the positive attitude toward life that the religion influences.

But this is not about that church or even about religiosity. It's about the church where I was organist for an even longer span of time — 16 years — at First Presbyterian in Santa Barbara.

And remember that I've been, until recently, organist in some church or other since I was 13. Amazingly, my first job as organist in Warrensburg, Missouri, was at — are you ready? — a Christian Science church that met in a small building, a house really, and the organ was a pump organ, so one's feet kept as busy as one's hands.

I was there only a few months and then was organist at my family church, First Christian — Disciples of Christ — where I sometimes convulsed one or two attendees with rather dissonant organ pieces I'd written.

When we lived in Kansas City, our church was Country Club Christian Church, a beautiful big building with an excellent organ. My mother always wanted me to be organist there, but we moved away and away, etc.

I usually had an "organ job" wherever I lived: a Lutheran church in New Haven, a Presbyterian church in Rochester, a Baptist and then Presbyterian church in Kansas City, Presbyterian and Lutheran churches in Arlington, and then Reformation Lutheran Church in Washington, D.C.. I've not played in a Temple, a Synagogue, would like to have.

While organist at these churches, I was also teaching, working as a composer, and have written about all that in other stories

And I've had lots of adventures, experiences in those churches, maybe to be expounded upon another time.

First Presbyterian in Santa Barbara! I became organist there in 1984 because the then-organist, David Hunsberger, phoned me and urged me to apply for the job (he was leaving, moving to the Bay Area).

So I did, and was hired. Julie Neufeld was appointed choir/music director at the same time, and we had a congenial several years working together. Julie was a precise, imaginative director, and allowed me to write quite a bit of music — for the choir, and for different soloists.

And the ministers: Larry Fisher, former minister who lived across the street with his wife, Ginger, and loved to hear the organ, and Rev. Bob Pryor and Mary Lou Pryor — wonderful people, and Rev. Peter Buehler — always a joy. And the amazing associate minister, Rev. Judith Muller. The heart of the church, along with the music.

Some of my best "church music" — anthems, solos — was written at First Presbyterian, and published, but mostly too different to appeal to "your" average choir director. And it was quite removed from the "praise" style of music that had become fashionable. *However,* I liked playing keyboard (Yamaha, electronic) with the "praise band" some of the time, enjoying adding embellishments to the harmony.

First Presbyterian Church in Santa Barbara. Emma Lou's favorite time as an organist was here

But the building itself, the great structure at State and Constance streets! The sanctuary seats several hundred and is one of the concert venues in Santa Barbara. The Choral

Society gives concerts there, and the Westmont College choirs and orchestra, and the Messiah "sing-along" takes place with the whole sanctuary, balcony, too, full of people.

The congregation singing at First Presbyterian in Santa Barbara

(Another plus for First Presbyterian: it has a good ventilation system. Some churches, especially older ones, acquire a distinctive odor if not aired out properly during the years.)

The church, the congregation, had moved from downtown to the present location in 1974, and the pipe organ was installed at the same time. It's the largest pipe organ in the area.

We replaced the four-manual Casavant console with a larger one built by Johannus that accommodated a fifth manual (keyboard) and some digital sounds (low pedal, strings, clarinet, harp, etc.) added to the original pipes. The fifth manual, the highest one, is used to play the small antiphonal division in the balcony.

There was a "period of adjustment" involving the synchronization of the digital and pipe sounds, but finally solved. Also, some organists had trouble reaching the top manual. I didn't, even though short (but skinny), and found it very useful.

I attached a sound box, a MIDI addition, that had many more sounds that could be programmed. And reverberation could be added to that and to the digital "stops" on the console to simulate the echo that some churches have to a high degree.

The late and indispensable David Techentin was the installer of the speakers in the pipe chambers to enhance the digital sounds. And he was the expert always with technical matters involving the organ.

The chapel has a digital organ, also from Johannus, that is a dream to make music on, with a speaker in the back of the room and others on either side of the altar. And reverb on the organ; there is nothing deader than an electronic organ without reverb. The chapel is a small, beautiful room, a lovely place to practice.

The main building, with the sanctuary in which the pipe organ resides, is designed with a cross extending along the entire ceiling, and the roof of the building outlines a giant cross that can be seen from the air.

I've always had a mystical feeling about buildings and the instruments inside — the organ of course, especially. It is a magical experience, to play the organ, to practice it early in the morning when you are alone, and to play for people to sing. And to write music on.

Yes, I know many churches don't have organs anymore. Pipe organs are quite expensive. *But if you can find someone to play it,* the organ can blend beautifully even with a praise band, believe it or not.

Also, digital organs with sampled sounds from organs in cathedrals all over the world are much less expensive than a pipe organ. There was, is a big battle about the introduction of electronics in organ sound, and I'll agree that there is *nothing* in the world like an acoustic pipe organ. But through necessity and invention the digital/electronic world has found its place, too. But no organ at all?....

"Amusing" that if you listened to radio soap operas or scary mysteries a long time ago, you heard a Hammond organ, a very versatile instrument that could provide percussive chords and mood music and jazzy rhythms; and if you studied the organ draw knobs, you'd learn about the harmonic series.

Before the tiny cells that determine frequencies in my inner ear became defective, I could love every sound from every rank of pipe and every combination of reeds and flutes and strings and diapasons from the slow beat of the slowest frequency of the lowest pedal sound to the highest mixtures of pitches from the very smallest pipes....

Candles, People, and Institutions

I have two things in my mind today.

One is putting to music the poem "Sea Fever" by John Masefield. I've been "setting it to music" mentally for some days and will write it down eventually. Is it modal? Does it change chord often? How much dissonance should it have? How high should it go? Does the meter stay the same? Should it have any graphic notation? Probably not.

The other "thing" is the town of Santa Barbara and what we remember about a town, a city. I think it is the people, and the institutions (an unromantic word for schools, churches, theatres).

Santa Barbara of course has the *ocean* and the *mountains*; they are why people come here. But there is the university!

When I first started teaching at UCSB, I taught an early morning theory class. At that hour, in the fall and winter, the campus would sometimes be enveloped by fog from the sea.

In my office, before going to class, I often lit a candle — not in any religious gesture. I didn't pray. I just liked the light and the cheer on a rather dark morning. I doubt that any of the other professors who had offices nearby (Bill Prizer, Peter Fricker, Ed Applebaum, Bob Freeman, Alejandro Planchart) lit candles. But I did.

And it reminds me of candles in another "institution" in town: Trinity Episcopal Church. It's the only Gothic building around. It was Philip Hubert Frohman's first structure in Gothic Revival Style. He later designed Washington National Cathedral (my favorite in all the world).

There is a kind of funny story about the prayer candles in Trinity. Near one of the entrances is an array of small candles that people come in and light and say a prayer in someone's memory. Marilyn (my friend who is a member of Trinity) said that one day a woman, off the street, not a member, came in and blew out all the candles. Marilyn saw her do this.

One could say all those prayers went up in smoke, but the candles were soon re-lighted by someone....

My friend and former student Barbara Hirsch, owner of Santa Barbara Yoga Center and founder of the classical recording studio in Santa Barbara, OPUS 1

Soon after I came to Santa Barbara two of the people I met right away were David and Carolyn Gell. David was organist at Trinity for many years and invited me to play on many of the organ recitals on the excellent pipe organ that inspired quite a few players and compositions. The Gells were extremely hospitable people. Carolyn is one of the people who I think is as near to being saintly (not in a dull sense) as one can be (the other was my sister Dorothy). You can define "saintly"; I define it as kind, generous, caring, interested, gracious, unselfish — all those good attributes.

The present organist, keyboard person and composer at Trinity is Tom Joyce, who is also a wonderful musician. I always love to hear Tom play, just as I did David.

At UCSB, I would sometimes go to the evening recitals given by students. I would drive in from my house in town and sit near the back of Lotte Lehmann Concert Hall, and was often the only faculty member of the few people in attendance. I had a fuzzy, white coat that felt warm on chilly evenings, and thinking back it must have looked a bit strange?, showy?, out of place?, and nothing to do with the story....

One of the students who always greeted me was Barbara Hirsch. Barb was in my theory classes and studied composition with me and later was a graduate student in composition. (Incidentally, when I was at UCSB at least half of the composition students were women, not the case in universities country-wide.) Barb also had a music program on KCSB-FM, the campus radio station, and became an expert in sound production and recording. After graduation she developed her own recording business and for many years has recorded all the symphony concerts and many other musical events in Santa Barbara.

So I'm proud of her and many other students who attended UCSB, a great institution.

Because you may be needing to do other things, I'll continue in another story about recordings and composing and people and such....

SECTION SIX
Observations, Unique Musical Entities and Happenings

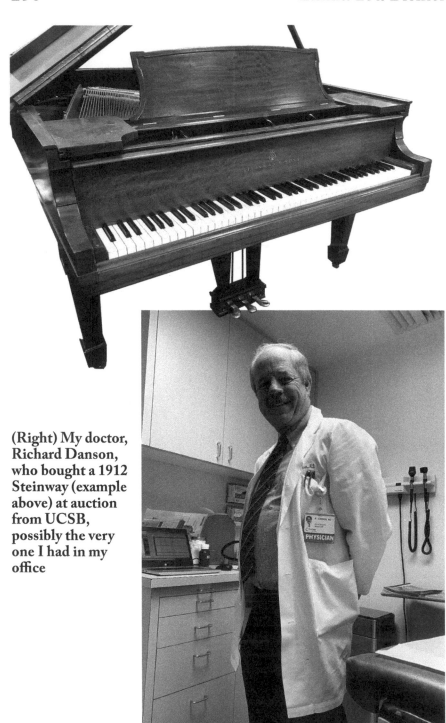

(Right) My doctor, Richard Danson, who bought a 1912 Steinway (example above) at auction from UCSB, possibly the very one I had in my office

My 1912 Steinway and a Doctor

A little story follows not having anything to do with coronavirus or politics (although we should be very aware and up-to-date on those matters).

When I was teaching at UCSB, I had in my office, for a few early years, a small spinet piano for teaching composition students and my occasional practice. One of the graduate student piano majors, John Clark, noticed this (bless grad students!), and somehow arranged for a 1912 Steinway grand to be moved into my office instead of the small piano. There is nothing like a Steinway, no matter what vintage.

Anyway, the other day on a more or less routine visit to my doctor, Richard Danson, the topic of pianos came up (it's always *so* nice when a doctor takes some interest in what a patient actually does, what profession the patient is in, rather than focusing only on the illness or wound or whatever brings them in) — and Dr. Danson said he has a 1912 Steinway piano in his home, one of the instruments that UCSB periodically auctions off for local purchase at a low price. He had no idea that it might have been my office piano at one time, and I didn't press the issue.

But if it is, I'm happy it is well-cared-for and appreciated. Just like one's life!

A Shining Light in Warrensburg, Missouri

I have written about Warrensburg, Missouri before. It is the city in which I lived 19 years. My memories are of my family, the people, the college (now University of Central Missouri), Hendricks Hall, the music store downtown (it was Burchfield's when I was there), the train station (now Amtrak), the cemetery (where all my family "reside"), the house in which we lived (Selmo Park, the College Residence, now gone). When I was there, the population was 5,000 and there were 16 churches, one of them First Christian where I was organist.

A light shines on all those memories, especially of course on my family. I have written about them, where we lived, the wheat fields that were almost surrounding the house when we first moved there, my father presiding over the college, my mother and grandmother, my sister, my twin brothers.

But there is another light now, one that I wasn't aware of until a few years ago. It shines on a place where pipe organs — pipe organs! — are built. The pipe organ is the most intricate musical instrument in existence. It is the most difficult to play. It is a wondrous creation.

Michael Quimby established the Quimby Pipe Organ Company — in Warrensburg! — in 1970. I find that miraculous.

When I lived in Warrensburg, there was the college, the most important entity, and the businesses in town, the many lovely homes — big and small. There were two major businesses that I remember: a shoe factory — and a slaughter house, of which we were quite aware on some days when the wind was in the right direction. I never visited either place, but they were part of the economics of the town.

Michael Quimby, owner Quimby Pipe Organ Company, Warrensburg, Missouri, showing off one of his creations at his plant.

Michael Quimby graduated from the college and was organist at the Methodist Church. And began to build pipe organs. You must read more about him.

I cannot get over the fact that a pipe organ, *a pipe organ!* — many of them — have been built, created there, in Warrensburg. Pardon me while I go into some sort of musical, vaporish paroxysm. A pipe organ is kind of a sacred "object" to those of us who play one. And to put one together takes genius of a special sort of dedication and knowledge — musical, technical, acoustical.

There are Quimby pipe organs in many churches now, prominent churches, smaller-but-cherished-churches.

And in Warrensburg, Missouri they are built. I wonder if the good citizens of the city know what a treasure is in their midst?

Golden Sounds

Edited by
Margo Halsted
Wesley Arai

For the 50th Anniversary of the UCSB Carillon
For Margo Halsted, UCSB Carillonist 2008-2018
For Wesley Arai, UCSB Carillonist 2018-

Emma Lou Diemer
2019

The metronome marking at the beginning is approximate, and further tempo indications should be flexibly interpreted at the discretion of the performer and in keeping with the characteristics of the instrument.

The observation of the fermatas is at the discretion of the performer and dependent up the dynamics and the instrument. Generally, the sound should almost die away before proceeding.

Bells

This article/essay/memoir is about *Bells*, so if you don't like bells, do not read it. Here is a song your grandmother/great-grandmother? Probably liked:

The bells of St. Mary's
Ah! hear they are calling
The young loves, the true loves
Who come from the sea
And so, my beloved
When red leaves are falling
The love bells shall ring out
Ring out for you and me
The bells of St. Mary's
At sweet even time
Shall call me, beloved
To come to your side
And out in the valley
In sound of the sea
I know you'll be waiting
Yes, waiting for me

A. Emmett Adams, music; Douglas Furber, lyrics.

It's a song my mother loved, from 1917. The movie with Bing Crosby came much later.

Most of all there is Poe's poem "The Bells", one of the most marvelously rhythmic poetic creations you'll ever read (try to keep your feet still or keep from dancing when you read it). Here is the first verse:

> *Hear the sledges with the bells —*
> *Silver bells !*
> *What a world of merriment their melody foretells !*
> *How they tinkle, tinkle, tinkle,*
> *In the icy air of night !*
> *While the stars that oversprinkle*
> *All the heavens, seem to twinkle*
> *With a crystalline delight ;*
> *Keeping time, time, time,*
> *In a sort of Runic rhyme,*
> *To the tintinnabulation that so musically wells*
> *From the bells, bells, bells, bells,*
> *Bells, bells, bells —*
> *From the jingling and the tinkling of the bells.*

We memorized it in junior high, thanks to our teacher, Pearl Bradshaw, in Warrensburg.

I of course set it to music, for the Arlington schools, for chorus and piano four hands. Boosey & Hawkes published it for awhile — it still should be.

(It's far more exciting than the Bing Crosby/Ingrid Bergman movie).

Back in Missouri we all knew about the bells in churches all over Belgium. Just before I left on a Fulbright Scholarship to study composition and piano in Brussels, my mother gave an all-afternoon reception with that theme, "Bells Over Belgium", complete with a centerpiece, a cut-out of a bell tower, on the dining table.

My first memories of the UCSB campus when I began a teaching career there were of the sounds of the carillon in Storke Tower, playing at intervals the "Let there be light" theme devised by faculty member Carl Zytowski. Those bells followed me all during the twenty teaching years and are still there to hear.

I wrote music for the various UCSB carillonists over the years, most recently for Wesley Arai, the present carillonist, and Margo Halsted, the outgoing carillonist who did so much to keep the carillon going and in good shape.

Several years ago I read that an Australian carillonist, June Catchpoole, had programmed a carillon piece of mine and had added my death date as 1996. I located her address and wrote that, no, that wasn't quite correct. The upshot was that I subsequently wrote several works for her and for other carillonists in Sydney and Canberra.

My first carillon piece had been for Margo Halsted for a collection she published celebrating the carillon in Leuven, Belgium.

The most recent is "Golden Sounds" for the 50th anniversary of the UCSB carillon.

And just now a short and merry trumpet/piano piece on "Ding Dong Merrily on High" for Isolde Weiermülle-Backes and Certosa Verlag.

The bells at UCSB are real bells, not electronic, and forces of nature...

> *Ding dong merrily on high,*
> *In heav'n the bells are ringing:*
> *Ding dong! verily the sky*
> *Is riv'n with angel singing*
> *Gloria Hosanna in excelsis!*
> *Gloria Hosanna in excelsis!*

A Euphonium

Boys Named Billy and Bill and a Musical Instrument

Oh dear, she's at her mini memoir again. One of my friend Marilyn's daughters calls them "cozy". Oh, well, they could be called worse things. I will soldier on.

When we lived in Kansas City (Missouri), I was born in our house on Edgevale Road and was in walking distance of J.C. Nichols school, which I attended as a young child. My playmates were the little boys and girls in that school and my best friends were some of the little boys. Why? They, at that time, were more active and adventuresome than the little girls. And four or five of the boys were named Billy. There was one boy who was called Bill. Bill was more serious and dignified than the ones called Billy. (Interesting how young children, all so different, can be remembered by their mien.)

The boy I played with most was Billy Pfeffer. On the vanity dresser in our house were two small figurine lamps made of porcelain. The figures were posed gracefully in flowing attire. One of the activities Billy Pfeffer and I liked to do was imitate the pose of those figures, as though in a play or dance (children must take to theatrics naturally, right?). Of course Billy and I played hide and seek with the other children and joined them in bruised knee roller skating. But I remember imitating the pose of the lamp figures best. The little lamps were in the family for years and my mother, before receptions, always had me turn them on along with other small lamps in the house.

When we moved to Warrensburg, I entered fifth grade
and became good friends with a brother and sister — Billy
and Joan (Jo-Ann) Turnbow. Joan had a lovely soprano
voice and so did Billy before his voice changed. They sang
beautiful duets in our church, First Christian. Billy and I
frequently played with other children in the snow on the
lawn in front of our house, Selmo Park. We often played
until twilight and dinnertime, our snow suits damp and
cold.

In high school Billy and I were in the school band,
playing nearly the same kind of instrument, Billy on
euphonium and I on baritone horn.

> (The main difference is the bore size. The
> euphonium is conical (the tubing gradually
> gets bigger from the mouthpiece to the bell)
> and the baritone is cylindrical (it maintains
> a consistent bore size throughout the major
> portion of the instrument which means it has
> a brighter sound). The baritone is considered
> a small bore instrument. It is pitched in BBb
> and typically has three valves. It is a traditional
> instrument of the British brass band. The
> euphonium has a larger bore (and is conical)
> and has a darker sound. Euphoniums will
> have three or four valves.) *Wikipedia*

Our band conductor, Mr. Losson, at first assigned
me trumpet, but soon baritone horn, an instrument that
often has a melody or countermelody in band pieces. My
music score had cues in small notes for other instruments;
and when those players were absent, Mr. Losson had me
play the cues, which made me feel important. Billy was
a little better player than I, but we were not really rivals,
and enjoyed playing the music back there with the other
brass. (The only thing I didn't like very much was marching
in our thin uniforms in the winter, I having to hold the
music with my left hand because I didn't have a little rack

attached to the instrument; but at that age such difficulties are a mere challenge.)

When I went to Yale, to the Music School, I knew no Billys or Bills or Williams. My friends were Michael Semanitsky and Armin Watkins and Don Katz (later Keats) and Nathan Gross and Robert Whittemore, mostly piano majors, although Don was a fellow composer. One of the sad parts of living a long life is losing friends like these.

One of my friends on *Facebook* is Frank Meredith, whom I have never met, and who is an outstanding player of low brass instruments and who suggested I write a piece for euphonium, which I did. It is a mostly lyrical, largely tonal work with a lingering in the mellow middle range of the instrument. I titled it "Halcyon Days", remembering those pleasant high school band experiences playing alongside Billy Turnbow.

It was a generally uncomplicated life and music was the center.

**French electronic music pioneer Maurice Martenot
and his Ondes Martenot in 1937**

The Essig Collection and the Theremin

W hen we moved from Kansas City (Missouri) to Warrensburg, I was nine years old. We attended many of the events at the college (now the University of Central Missouri), events that were held in Hendricks Hall.

One of those events remains vividly in my memory years later. It was the presentations/concerts put on by the Essig Troup. I remember it especially because my sister Dorothy and brother George were musicians in the Troup. Both of them were students in the college as was our brother John. John was an excellent musician, too, but I particularly remember Dorothy and George playing instruments in the concerts. (Many of the instruments were wind-produced; Dorothy was a flutist, George was a cornetist.)

Don Essig was the developer/founder of the bands at the college and had amassed a collection of over 400 instruments, unusual/strange/weird/amazing/beautiful, and some of these were played at the concerts. Mr. Essig would introduce and talk about them.

(The collection is housed in Kirkpatrick Library on the university campus at the McClure Archives and University Museum. Patricia Smith, who lives in Warrensburg and whose father was Dean of the College at one time, will know more about this.)

The instruments, sound makers, included brass and wind and percussion and the one that I best recall seeing and hearing played and what this article is mostly about:

It was a theremin. You can look up the history of this early electronic instrument. It has been used in the music scores of many motion pictures (including Hitchcock's *Spellbound*) and can produce an eerie or beautiful succession of pitches and gradations of volume by the movement of the hands of the player. It is the only instrument that is not touched by the performer.

Composers who have used it include Oliver Messiaen, who also used the Ondes Martenot, a similar instrument but one that has a keyboard.

I mention the theremin because here is another instance of a marvel of invention and ingenuity that the people of Warrensburg and the college — and children like me, at the time — could experience without going to Europe or big cities or other places of renown, and remember.

Alexandra Stepanoff playing the theremin on NBC Radio, 1930

Emma Lou and Betty Ann Davidson, accompanying for a recital in the music room of Selmo Park on the Vose Grand (c 1943)

Pianos

The *Piano!* When you were a child, was there a piano in your home? One hopes so. They are wondrous instruments. In my house in Warrensburg, thanks to my parents and all the gods that be, there was one — a small "Vose" (have you heard of that make?), a sweet grand piano that all of us played.

The one pictured in my house in Santa Barbara (and excuse the messy room) came into my possession some years ago when the then-owner of Santa Barbara Music told me he had a piano that had been used/played for five years around town by visiting artists and that I could buy it for a drastically low price.

I had always wanted a concert grand — who hasn't? — and said yes. We made sure the floor in the living room would support it and we had five men move it in.

The grand piano is such a beautiful object; some people have one just for its beauty — but there is always the hope that someone will learn to play it. (Once a new neighbor came in and saw our piano and asked if it were just for show. I ripped off a few cadenzas — there was the "show".).

You don't need a 9-foot grand for writing music.

If you've gone to music school, you've played all manner of pianos.

I remember that at Yale one entered Sprague Hall and on the left was the door down to the women's rest room and in the rest room was a door leading out to a large conglomeration of practice rooms and various spaces for students to meet and chat.

Each practice room had a little window in the door that you could look through and see if the piano was occupied and who was playing it. Some pianists covered up the window so they couldn't be spied on.

I had a friend (Nathan Gross) who, when I was absorbed in practicing, would flip the door handle outside loudly and scare me in mid-phrase.

And the practice rooms at Eastman, like Yale, had small, upright pianos, some with cigarette burns on a few keys — that was long ago.

The point is, one can practice on and create music on any keyboard instrument, preferably one with 88 keys or more or less.

The Steinway in Emma Lou's home in Santa Barbara

Piano has been my main instrument/first love/music inspirer for all the years. There was a scare some years ago with the advent of synthesizers — Moog, etc. — when it was predicted the *Piano* would be obsolete, replaced by patch cords and plug-ins and all manner of electronically-produced sounds not of much interest to us who were keyboard people. Playing on a keyboard is half the fun.

Finally, keyboards were added to synthesizers and then people like me became interested.

And electronic pianos and harpsichords and organs. You can tell the difference — amplify anything, make it electronic instead of acoustic, and there is a difference. An acoustic piano does not have to be amplified, though we've done it and had instruments and human voices played, sung into it (with piano pedal depressed) for echo effects.

Some composers did not, do not, play the piano. It determines, if you're not careful, patterns that persist, "pianistic" patterns in keeping with the technical skill of the composer. Think Rachmaninoff and his big left-hand-*arpeggios*.

But the mystique of the piano and music composed on and for it allowed Schumann and Brahms and Chopin and Liszt to become famous. Of course they wrote music for other mediums, but if you are a pianist you remember them for their music you played.

Many of us like to have privacy when we are practicing or writing music. In a music school environment, with many pianists practicing, you feel as though what you are playing won't be heard in the bedlam. When you live in an apartment or house, you hope the neighbors won't hear you (unless you want them to).

Didn't Beethoven move 17 times in Vienna? Was that because he played loudly, trying to hear what he was playing?

A piano concerto is the epitome of piano music. I wrote a piano concerto for Betty Oberacker and she premiered it with the Santa Barbara Symphony (and it later received a Kennedy Center Friedhelm award and she performed it in the competition at the Kennedy Center — it didn't win top prize, but at least "placed", and received a standing ovation). I wrote an earlier piano concerto that hasn't really been performed except as part of a doctoral student's dissertation.

The *Saint-Saëns Organ Symphony* (*Symphony No. 3 in C minor, Op. 78*) was also played in Santa Barbara. I was the organist, playing the Robert Morton theatre organ in the Arlington Theater. I believe it was the only time that organ was used with the symphony — worth another article.

If you've seen that *Saint-Saens* symphony performed, you know that the organist must sit motionless on the organ bench for what seems hours before entering very quietly. When we rehearsed, the conductor, Varujan Kojian, wanted the organ quieter, but I was using the softest stop on the organ. An orchestra member, I think it was the principal cellist, Geoffrey Rutkowski, explained that the organ couldn't be made any softer. There is a place in the second movement where the organ suddenly enters fortissimo on a C major chord, and it's always great fun to see the audience jump in terror.

But getting back to the piano, I've written a lot for it — easy music, difficult music — and will write about that.

Stravinsky apparently composed much of his music at the piano. We can imagine that the percussive capability inspired the punctuated chords in his *Rite of Spring*, as well as the lyrical harmonies toward the end of *The Firebird*.

Niece Theresa Augsburger Tabi and her daughter Ayla play a piano-flute duet at Emma Lou's Santa Barbara home

The Church of the Holy Spirit in Heidelberg, Germany

When Practicing in Church can be Scary

Here's another story to distract us (me) from developing events. The story is a little scary, being about practicing in a dark church at night, particularly women organists doing this. (Men can be in danger, too, of course; a good friend of mine was attacked one night after organ practice in Rochester — he survived, thank God.).

I have several incidents. I should add that I rarely practiced at night; my favorite time was very early in the morning before the office opened. I like to not bother people; in one church I played, the office was next to the sanctuary. But especially, I don't want to be heard.

However, I learned that the former minister of First Presbyterian Santa Barbara, Rev. Larry Fisher, who lived with Mrs. Fisher across the street from the church, would hear the organ in the early morning and "sneak" in and sit in a back pew to listen. I was oblivious to this until years later, after his death. Mrs Fisher (Ginger) told me of her husband's love of the organ. We know not who is listening.

A few scary stories: when I was in high school I went one evening to practice at my church and became aware of a man coming into the choir loft where the organ console was located. In a small town one knows most of the people and I did not recognize this man, who looked suspicious. I (I like to think "coolly") turned off the organ and left. Maybe he started playing the organ; I know not.

Also, years later, I was to give a Sunday recital at my church in SB and got into town Saturday evening, from a trip, and went directly to the church. (My niece Betty told me that when she had to practice at night, her husband, Larry, went along, and my friend Marilyn has been known to "stand guard" for me here sometimes.) Anyway, I got into the church through the sacristy and turned on *all* the lights in the sanctuary, balcony, narthex, and all. No heads popped up from the pews, there was not a sound. Soon I was absorbed in playing and forgot all about anyone who might be there. Sorry to disappoint you — there was no one, and I had a good practice there alone. Our fears are imagined, most of the time.

However, we took a trip to Heidelberg, Germany one summer to a women composers' conference. Marilyn's daughter and her husband and children came from Norway to see us/visit. An incident on that trip involved their 2-year-old son falling into a fountain pool and being rescued by a quick-thinking gentleman.

But on to the organ recital of music by women composers I was to give at the cathedral, a reverberant, beautiful stone edifice whose pipe organ had stops and buttons that lit up at the touch. (This was in the 80s, and I had never seen this extremely useful feature before, though it is common now.)

The only practice time I was given was quite late at night, and the music director gave me a key. I let myself in about midnight and reveled in the spaciousness and echoing splendor of the cathedral. But it was a Saturday night, and soon I heard bottles being thrown against the outside walls of the building, the sounds of breaking glass echoing throughout the nave. (I thought a bit about the ominous remnants of Nazi Germany). But, as is my wont, I set about practicing the amazing, rather discordant music for the concert. One becomes lost in the music, indeed.

Suddenly, after an hour or so, I was aware of a man standing next to the organ...here, really ominous music could be added...but to make you relax I must tell you it was one of the young organists of the cathedral, come to accompany me back to my hotel. Sorry folks; it isn't Hitchcock.

SECTION SEVEN
More About Music

(Left) The poet Alice Meynell, 1847-1922, who was the inspiration for some of Emma Lou's music (below) such as "Four Poems"

Alice Meynell

In the 1970s I wrote quite a bit of music — whenever not? — and a poet I discovered was Alice Meynell. Be sure to look her up. I would think she is one of the Romantic poets. She was an active suffragette, editor, mother of eight children, etc. And some of her poetry is heartbreakingly moving, like:

Renouncement
I must not think of thee; and, tired yet strong,
I shun the love that lurks in all delight—
The love of thee—and in the blue heaven's height,
And in the dearest passage of a song.
Oh, just beyond the sweetest thoughts that throng
This breast, the thought of thee waits hidden yet bright;
But it must never, never come in sight;
I must stop short of thee the whole day long.
But when sleep comes to close each difficult day,
When night gives pause to the long watch I keep,
And all my bonds I needs must loose apart,
Must doff my will as raiment laid away, —
With the first dream that comes with the first sleep
I run, I run, I am gather'd to thy heart."

And this one:

Chimes
Brief, on a flying night,
From the shaken tower,

A flock of bells take flight,
And go with the hour.
Like birds from the cote to the gales,
Abrupt—O hark!
A fleet of bells set sails,
And go to the dark.
Sudden the cold airs swing.
Alone, aloud,
A verse of bells takes wing
And flies with the cloud.

(You can imagine that sets off a composer's mind, if you like bells.)

I had two different commissions in the 70s and set these two poems and several others of hers. One commission was from Mu Phi Epsilon for solo voice and chamber ensemble. It was performed at a Mu Phi convention in Kansas City. The other was from Dickinson State College and was for chorus and chamber ensemble. The first one was published by Carl Fischer and must be moldering in their vaults. The other one is in my file drawer — someone from Dickinson asked about it, had come across it, several years ago.

Such is the fate of some of our best work. Alice Meynell never knew I set seven of her poems (she died in 1922), but we owe our inspiration to poets like her, whether forgotten or not.

Here is another that called for music:

My Fair, no beauty of thine will last
My Fair, no beauty of thine will last
Save in my love's eternity.
Thy smiles, that light thee fitfully,
Are lost for ever--their moment past--
Except the few thou givest to me.
Thy sweet words vanish day by day,
As all breath of mortality;
Thy laughter, done, must cease to be,

And all thy dear tones pass away,
Except the few that sing to me.
Hide then within my heart, oh, hide
All thou art loth should go from thee.
Be kinder to thyself and me.
My cupful from this river's tide
Shall never reach the long sad sea.

I think many people prefer happy poetry, but in some periods of one's life or one's day it is the melancholy poems that speak the loudest. I set these poems to music during the final months of illness of my friend, Phyllis King.

Creativity

I'm not a student of child psychology or any kind of psychology, but believe most children like to be creative. And when they are adults, too. We have a neighbor who makes quilts. She gives them to her grandchildren or charitable organizations. Or she just hangs them in her house to enjoy.

My favorite person at church was Jeannette Klingler (who played the piano beautifully until she was 102), and made gorgeous quilts.

In my own family, I saw some childhood sketches that my mother had done of a building — neat, very ordered.

My father wrote books on education.

My brother John built things — I remember a desk he designed and constructed in college.

My sister wrote poetry.

My mother and grandmother crocheted, knitted, sewed.

People who design gardens are creative. Architects are.

What makes a person want to create?

"…is the Maker of heaven and earth, the sea, and everything in them…". I don't fathom that concept, but I surely like those things that were created by some force, and the biblical explanation is a lot more poetic than the "big bang theory".

My "tools" in writing music are hands on the piano, at least were in the beginning.

There was music paper around because my brothers wrote arrangements for their dance band. I drew notes on the music paper sometimes — just to make markings on the lines.

And then I tried to make sense of the sounds I was inventing. There was no order or reason at first, until I imitated what I had heard or played — music that was put together in an orderly way.

In my early teens I wrote two "piano concertos", having spent hours listening to those by Grieg and Tchaikovsky. They are lost; they were very imitative. But a beginning. And exciting. Do not discourage a young creator's efforts because they are imitative at first.

One day I broke away entirely from tonality and wrote a piece in which I didn't repeat notes right away, was rather atonal. My teacher said "Where did that come from?".

In the beginning we used pencil and paper, then copied our scores on vellum with Higgins black ink and had them reproduced. I had an electric eraser or white-out to make changes. It was messy, but it may have been better than all the music I've written sitting at the computer the last several years. And how interesting are computer print-outs in an archive? Not very.

I find that to get a really good idea I need to play the piano or organ or synthesizer, improvise, as I used to when composing — and only that. Several times I've connected the clavinova to the computer and improvised into a music program and edited it and printed it out. I don't think that a composer has been able to record an improvisation and see it notated before c.1985? — something like that ....

organ

EMMA LOU DIEMER

for
Percussion and Organ
(*or Piano*)

organ and two percussionists
(three perc. Psalm 67)

for
Joan DeVee Dixon
Michael Matteo
Brian Tychinski
Scott Sexton

commissioned by
Alvin C. Broyles

C. Alan
publications

CAP 0333

Composing Music

Oh, no! Here she is again. This time I'm going to write about composing music — when, why, for whom, that sort of thing. And don't read it if you are really tired of the "me-ness", the examined life of someone else, the indulgent use of the captive *Facebook*.

But this minor composer has a lot to say, and who better to say it than the composer? After all, Berlioz wrote his *Mémoires*; why shouldn't I?

My most recent piece, written a few weeks ago, was a piece for euphonium and piano. Why did I write it? Two reasons:

1) Frank Meredith, whom I had never met, hinted that I should write something for euphonium.

I've since gotten acquainted with Frank through his very amusing and informative book *Life in the Pits* that you can read on kindle. He has had a fascinating life as a brass player, particularly bass trombone, and euphonium.

2) I played baritone horn in the school band all through high school. It is very close in sound and playing to the euphonium, which is conical; the baritone is cylindrical. I had always wanted to write for it, and Frank gave me an excuse.

Just before that piece or about the same time, I wrote a suite for piano, four hands for the wonderful duo pianists, Tachell Gerbert and Bradley Gregory. They were students at UCSB of Wendell Nelson, and I've written for them before.

The title of the euphonium piece is "Halcyon Days".
The title of the piano four hands work is *By the Sea*:

> *By the sea, by the sea, by the beautiful sea,*
> *you and I, you and I, oh how happy we'll be...*
> *by the seaside, the beautiful sea...*

(Shouldn't that be "you and me, you and me..."? Oh, well.)

The suite is based on that popular song written in 1914. Neither of these works has been performed yet, thanks to the virus, but will be.

I've written a great deal of music for the organ. Why? I've been a church organist since the age of 13, but didn't begin to write music for organ until I was almost out of college (Yale), being more interested in piano music, but decided to write music for organ that I could play in church.

I played some of the early pieces in my church in Warrensburg and my mother said the dentist who sat across the aisle thought I was making mistakes and, I'm sure, grimaced noticeably. My mother always related people's reactions, not always favorable.

I wrote some big pieces with a reverberant cathedral sound in mind, and played them in recitals in D.C. and other places, and I wrote one or two collections of hymn tune settings.

Dale Wood, noted church composer and editor, was aware of these and asked me to write some settings of old, 19th century hymn tunes. I did, and every year afterward, until his death, I sent him a new collection that he published. *Preludes to the Past. With Praise and Love. Carols for Organ.* etc.

I wasn't interested in writing Bach-like settings, or overly contrapuntal, canonic treatments, but rather mood pieces that tried to express the words and were a bit different in the use of melodic development, harmonies, rhythms.

A reviewer of one of the first collections — pre-Dale Wood — *Seven Hymn Preludes* — disparaged the use of *ostinato*, repeated figures (hello, Philip Glass, years later).

Another reviewer, of the rhythmic settings — *Folk Hymn Sketches* — criticized them, expounded that they would be better heard in a shopping mall. I wrote to him: "Where? When?".

One of the major organ works I wrote later in life was *Four Biblical Sketches*. It was commissioned for one of the American Guild of Organists regional conventions, and Sandra Soderlund premiered it. It is probably my best organ work. A couple of other people have played it (and a German organist, just last week, took an interest in it; will wonders never cease?).

Joan DeVee Dixon, who knew about my collection *Psalms for Percussion and Organ*, wrote to me about writing more psalm settings, and she began to commission me to write works for organ solo and for organ and various instruments (trumpet, flute, trombone, percussion, brass ensemble).

Over a period of a few years I set nearly all the psalms for these combinations, commissioned by Joan and her husband, Alvin Broyles. She also asked me to write a concert piece on Alvin's favorite hymn, "Abide With Me", and he heard it before his death. The piece is in 19th century style harmonically and quite big, and loud, virtuosic (not your quiet funereal "Abide With Me").

In writing these works for Joan I composed either at the piano, or organ, or Yamaha keyboard. At one point, needing to have some privacy, I took a small keyboard into the blower room at church (the organ blower wasn't on) to write.

I'll write about other works — orchestra, choral next. Once a composer, always a composer....

Much of Emma Lou's composing was done at home on either her Steinway, seen from above (top) or her Yamaha keyboard (right).

Delaying Tactics in Music Writing

I'm supposed to be writing music right now, specifically a jazzy fugue for three string instruments. As usual, when writing a piece at this more advanced age, I procrastinate and think of lots of other things to do like empty the waste baskets or check the email.

Of course when I first began writing music, there were certainly no email or computers or even electronic pianos. And not much procrastination, if any. I wrote on an acoustic piano (no amp, no echo, just the sound of hammers striking the strings and the pitches and the wonderful resonance the "loud" pedal produced). It was easy to write at the piano, a natural setting and unique sound and untold possibilities of color and flamboyance and invention.

The computer is no match, but here I am writing a fugue at the Apple iMac and hearing an imperfect playback of distorted string sound and pitch. Luckily, in one's head is the actual sound of strings and musical notes or all would be lost.

And as one's age advances — imperceptibly, intriguingly — one does procrastinate a bit, as you can see. It has to do with some diminishment of energy, and some laziness. And too many distractions?

But music-writing has always been the joy, an eagerly-looked-forward-to activity, really the "reason for being". So I'd better get to it: figure out that second counter-subject and the compositional device where the escape from academic-ism can occur. It will be in the episodes where there will be touches of "bluegrass" or pentatonic ebullience. Let there be rhythm. Bach is brimming with rhythm!

I've always hated it when people *talk* about music or *write about* it instead of playing it — or writing it!

So after this break it will be a relief to get back to that off-beat fugue subject and the development that's called for and some attention to and sympathy for the listeners and the players.

Let the music continue! Are you listening?

Electronic Music

Electronic music turns some people off though those of us who are well-acquainted with electronic organs and some film scores should feel at home with it as a medium.

There were students at UCSB who knew more about wave forms and amplitude and frequency modulation — and multi-track recording and amplification and sound placement — than I did. There was Doug Scott and Terry Setter and David Barton and others who helped set up and run the electronic music studio. When we got somewhat into computer music, there were no easy systems. Analog. Digital.

Also there was *musique concrete*, which was not electronic, but bell sounds or voices or doors squeaking that could be combined with electronic sounds and manipulated to the point that one could not really recognize the original source.

When I hear a sound played backward, which happens on one of the radio program announcements, I know what it is (the decay is first, and then sustain, and then attack — weird and discomfiting, but I've even created it, in early tape maneuvers).

One of the machines that I had in 1986 was a sampler, and I went to the church and recorded some chords on the pipe organ and worked them into a composition called "Church Rock" by creating a tape with the sampled sounds on several tracks with which I could improvise on a real pipe organ.

I played it on a program once at National City Christian Church in Washington, D.C. (where Lawrence Schreiber was organist at the time and was compliant), and the church had loud speakers all over the sanctuary and when the tape played, it was "surround sound" and even echoing in the space.

The piece was divided into different sections that had different moods — some rhythmic, some chorale-like — and my "score" was comprised of directions as to the style in which to play: "sharp chords", "folk melody line", "quiet and mysterious".

The electronic pieces I created at home were four-track, the four speakers placed around the room, and each improvised track was overlaid with another improvisation. Since electronic sounds are limitless, there had to be some careful selection — something like choosing registration on an organ.

So I had "patches", sounds that were created from the various wave forms and manipulated, had them enumerated, and the score was those numbers that I had placed in a certain order. One track might be background sound and the next punctuated interpolations, clusters even.

I wrote a couple of anthems that had a tape part (a few composers have done that), and of course some instrumental works with tape.

For one Sunday service at the church where I was organist (First Presbyterian), I devised an all-electronic music service. It wasn't especially popular.

Milton Babbitt came to UCSB to lecture one time, and the audience had a fair number of professors from the sciences since he was known as an early expert in the computer field.

Are composers moved by hearing their own electronic music? Once, at a computer music conference that I attended, one of Babbitt's works was played (from recording) and I could see he had tears in his eyes afterward.

2   Do You Know the Land

For the Monte Vista High School Concert Choir, Danville, California.
Bruce Koliha, Conductor

A DREAM WITHIN A DREAM

For Mixed Voices, S.A.T.B., with Piano

EDGAR ALLAN POE (1809-1849)   EMMA LOU DIEMER

Moving quietly ♩ = 70

Favorite Medium

My favorite medium for writing music is chorus and orchestra, and if organ is thrown in, so much the better. And the words one is setting to music are the inspiration. A close second favorite is the art song.

I've never written an opera. I guess I would like to, but have reservations, the lack of an inspiring *libretto* being only one. A composer I admire greatly is Brahms, who never wrote an opera. He poured his genius into piano music and symphonies and songs and chamber music and never wrote a note that didn't ring true, like Bach.

A musical — that would be fun to write. It's the songs you remember, not really the stage cluttered with people and action. The music.

If music — and the words — are the thing, not the scenery nor the acting nor the plot — then it is the most important element and does not need distraction from it. I'm very fond of films and sometimes find the film score of great interest, but become more often involved with the visual, the action, and forget about the music. Some of the best films have no score at all.

Granted it takes a great deal of talent to write a "good" opera. But so does a cantata. Or an art song.

Music itself, and poetry — there is the magic.

For choruses, singers, choirs over the course of years I've set to music texts from (are you ready?):

The Bible, Walt Whitman, Shakespeare, Thomas Campion, Edgar Allan Poe, Ogden Nash, Dorothy Parker,

Emily Dickinson (especially Emily Dickinson—who hasn't?), Mary Oliver, Dorothy Diemer Hendry, Sarah Teasdale, Edna St. Vincent Millay, Kabir, John Donne, Robert Louis Stevenson, Edmund Spenser, Alice Meynell, James Joyce, Edward Lear, Omar Khayyam, Henry Timrod, Archibald Rutledge, May Sarton, Sister Mary Virginia Micka, Hildegard von Bingen, Christina Rossetti, Alfred Lord Tennyson, William Blake, Sir Walter Scott, Peter Cornelius, John Milton, Ida Coolbrith, Thomas Mordaunt, Oscar Wilde, Helen Skinner Anderson, Robert Herrick, Flannery O'Connor, Amy Lowell, William Byrd, Paul Willis, Fred Pratt Green, Anabel Miller, Martin Luther, Oliver Wendell Holmes, Richard Leach, Christopher Webber, Pablo Neruda, Catherine de Vinck, Christopher Marlowe, Robert Lowell, Johann Goethe, Flannery O'Connor, Molly Katherine Cornett (b. 2002), Zoe Johnson (b. 2005), and some I can't locate.

There are others, a few, I wasn't able to get permission to use: an excerpt from "The Little Prince" and a poem by Thomas Wolfe, though I'm sure some composers have.

Setting texts to music is about the easiest thing a composer (I) can do. The mood is there, the beauty of the words, the rhythm, the form.

I like poetry that asks to be set to music — the first line, the atmosphere, the imagery, not preachy, not wordy, not too incomprehensible or depressing. Like this, by Goethe:

> *Do you know the land where the lemon-trees grow,*
> *in darkened leaves the gold-oranges glow,*
> *a soft wind blows from the pure blue sky,*
> *the myrtle stands mute, and the bay-tree high?*
> *Do you know it well?*
> *It's there I'd be gone,*
> *to be there with you, O, my beloved one!*

Improvising

I just put another improvisation on *Facebook*. Don't ask me why I did that. Oh, I know; we all know: performers like to perform. Sometimes there is an urge to play, to improvise. It's how we composers began to compose — at least I think most of us began that way. We became note-readers along the way, out of necessity because we were taking lessons, and we were curious, and teachers don't usually look kindly on improvs, rather than the learning of an assigned piece of music.

Now in this twilight — of what? The world? Civilization? The USA? Me? — one has an impulse to play that music-maker, that sounds-producing instrument waiting in the living room.

It's the twilight of reading music as well as in one's earlier years. The light is bad, one has trouble seeing the score, one has played all that before, So it is easier sometimes to improvise, dispense with the dim notes, play something somewhat new, which an improv is.

I don't improvise in a jazz style — I guess I could, but I'd rather hear an expert do it. I've gotten in the habit of playing pop melodies (embellishing them) that come to mind. And patriotic ones, hymns. melodies that my mother played and sang. But embellished to the point of recognizability, varying and developing them.

An improv doesn't have a plan or it shouldn't. It should be spur-of-the-moment. Whether anyone else enjoys it is a tiny bit beside the point. "Created on the spot, without preparation" — those are the criteria.

No doubt Bach improvised fugues. I can't do that. I don't have the mind of Bach (no one has). I can use some imitation, some polyphony, but mostly I probably improvise more the way Debussy or Ravel (oh, I wish!) may have: harmonies, pianistic patterns, new combinations of chords, bits of melody. The wider the vocabulary one has, the more interesting the improvisation.

The one I just put on *Facebook* was just an impulse — no preparation, just working in a few "tunes" — and needs more rhythmic interest, and I may do one later that has that. Each improvisation is different (unless one runs out of ideas or had very few to begin with).

I don't hear any clamoring for other improvs — most people would rather hear a little Brahms, some Mozart, a Beatles tune — oh, well, it is fun, good for the fingers and the soul, and the Steinway becomes lonely sitting there with no one playing it, and the virus looming outside and the riots/rallies/protests everywhere. Music protests if it is not made, listened to. So be prepared!

Librarians and Prokofiev

In this time of plague and in the wee hours of the morning it's nice to think about people and music.

Chris Husted always has something interesting on his page. He worked with Martin Silver at one time. Martin was the music librarian at UCSB during my tenure there, and he knew where every music score and book was, as does Temmo Korisheli, present librarian.

Librarians seem to be multi-talented. One of the daughters (Ann) of my friend Marilyn is a librarian and also an artist and writes poetry. Martin Silver played the flute; Temmo is a singer and choral director.

Some years ago I ran into Chris and Martin at a concert at the Lobero Theatre. Computer/internet language was coming into practice and in our discussion I pretended to know something about HTTP and PDF and all the rest about which I know very little (I had to ask a composer friend a few years ago how to create a PDF).

On musical ground I'm a bit more literate. I wrote in a previous "essay" that my mother's favorite piece was Chopin's "Ballade in F major"; she liked the other three ballades, too, but especially this one, the second one. It begins innocuously and liltingly and then all hell breaks loose, and Chopin plays with both of these concepts (peace and conflict?) until the end, a genius of dramatic development of ideas.

My personal favorite work is Prokofiev's *Seventh Sonata*. It has a tempestuous third movement in 7/8 that

Russian Composer Sergei Prokofiev c 1918

is relentless in its energy and drive. Once I went with my organ teacher, Edna Billings, to hear Horowitz play this major work and Mrs. Billings found it terrifying (the way Horowitz could sometimes almost lose control, but not really, but pretty much resort to banging). I played the Prokofiev last movement at Yale for my pianist friend, Armin Watkins, and he hoped I would play it on the fairly light-actioned piano in Sprague Hall before the heavier-action instrument would be brought in. (I did.)

Listeners hear music differently: I might be mentally analyzing the chords and use of motives in a piece such as the Prokofiev and someone else might be imagining a storm at sea.

A composer gathers together ideas, chooses which ones to use, arranges them in some sort of loose or strict order, adds a lot of emotional color (if he or she is so inclined and capable) and produces either a work of art or another mediocre piece.

I may now go and think up some musical motives and see what becomes of them. This time of plague should produce something terrifying — or peaceful?

Thrill-ing us with glad sur-prise. Glo-ry, Glo-ry, be to God

For a song of love *di-ur-nal! Glo-ry, Glo-ry, be to God

For a song of Love

NMP-360

* Meaning ready or recurring
** Substitute the names of the Bride and

for Deanna Jean Augsburger and Edwin Dudley Burwell IV
May 4, 2002

17

Wedding Song
for solo voice and keyboard

Dorothy Diemer Hendry, 2002   Emma Lou Diemer, 2002

With a lilting joy ♩ = 160 *(or a bit slower)*   *lightly, a bit detached*

Dear friends of the bride, dear friends of the groom, God

bless you for com-ing to-day. *and shar-ing the hope of a life-time of love as

joy-ful as rose-buds in May. as joy-ful as rose-buds in May.

*The bride's and groom's names may be substituted here: e.g.
'and giving Deanna and Eddie your love", etc.

Occasional Music

We composers, in a lifetime, are asked to write many different kinds of works for special occasions. In my own composing history, these are sometimes commissions with $$ attached, sometimes "pro bono". (And sometimes we write something just because we want to.)

Special occasions can be a wedding, graduation, concert tour, anniversary, retirement, memorial, inauguration, friendship. And sometimes writing a work "just because we want to" produces the most innovative music. But I'll write about some "special occasions".

My biggest commission, some years ago, was from a man wanting an organ piece written in honor of his wife. The resulting work was ok, not really world-shaking, not "one of my best", but it was accepted graciously by both of them. (It was published)

Another, a special occasion, rather amusing, took place in one of the high schools in Arlington, VA when I was composer-in-residence in the county schools a long time ago. I was asked to write a graduation processional for the seniors in one of the schools. I was organist for the event so the ceremony must have been in a church although I seem to remember an auditorium (did any of the schools there have an organ? Did any school anywhere have one? I believe one of the high schools in Santa Barbara had an organ at one time).

Wherever it was, I wrote a processional — celebratory, rather march-like, happy. The morning of the graduation I played some prelude music and watched for the students to gather at the entrance door. Finally, I saw them lined up, waiting to march in. So I began to play the piece I had written for them. No one moved. They stood there, waiting. Finally, in desperation, I finished off the piece and started playing "Pomp and Circumstance", the usual processional for many a graduation. Then they moved, began to march in. I know not what happened later to that piece I wrote. Elgar reigned!

There were many choral commissions during those years, choral directors wanting to have a work like the *Three Madrigals*. Such a work's "essence" was never to happen again, even with Shakespeare's assistance, but one tries. (You can never "go home again!").

Usually, always, after I did write something for the commissioner who probably wanted another *Three Madrigals*, I would receive a thank-you letter of appreciation — how pleased they were, how perfect, how beautiful.

But once I wrote a short setting of an Elizabethan text and gave it a rhythm I liked for poems of that era. I sent it to the choral director who had commissioned it. And never heard a word. No response. Nada. The work was published and I see it is "online" and apparently available. 1'35" duration. Oh, well.

I found, with experience, that when a commissioner asked me what the fee should be, it was better for me to say something like "whatever is allocated in your budget" or "whatever you think reasonable in comparison to other commissions you've made". I know that sounds unprofessional. Some established, or semi-established composers "charge" so much a minute. *However*, I discovered that if I mentioned a certain amount or range it was invariably lower than what was ultimately offered and paid. Of course remember: it's not the $$; it's the product that matters?

Of course I wrote wedding music for brides and grooms at First Presbyterian in Santa Barbara: Susan and Mark, Judith and David, Carol and Thomas. What is more joyful than a wedding?

As for other "no fee" occasional music, 2002 was a productive year for the collaboration between my poet sister Dorothy and myself. We wrote two wedding songs, one for a great niece, Jessicah, in Philadelphia and one for one of Dorothy's grandchildren, Deanna, in Huntsville, Alabama. Also a Lullaby for one of Dorothy's great-grandchildren, Ayla, in Austin, Texas.

And we wrote a hymn for the 125th anniversary of First Presbyterian in Warrensburg, Missouri. This was at the instigation of Conan Castle, the music director. The celebration was a year or so after the diagnosis of Dorothy's terminal illness. She was confined at home and I made the trip to the celebration alone. I remember feeling like an honored representative of our writer/composer team, and some sweet sadness when the hymn was sung and when I visited Sunset Hill Cemetery where the rest of our family is buried.

"Welcome to This Holy Church" is the title of the hymn. Composers are allowed to give new hymns a "hymn tune" name, and we/I named it *Warrensburg*. Other tune names I've bestowed on other hymns I've written are *Santa Barbara* for "For the Fruit of All Creation" that appeared in the 1978 Lutheran hymnal. And *Reformation* for a new tune for Martin Luther's "Eine Feste Burg" text written for Church of the Reformation in Washington, D.C..

Quality vs. Quantity

But, really, since "quality" is a very subjective judgment, this is only about "quantity". Or is it?

Quantity being the number of words or pages or notes or duration of something. Duration of a musical work — there's the proper subject?

One of the most beloved of Chopin's preludes, the one in E minor, is only a few measures. Of course it is the easiest (one can debate that because playing a lovely melody successfully may not be easy), but the beginning pianist chooses it because there are fewer notes. It is also beautiful (don't debate that) with a downward repeated-chord progression and a plaintive, almost static melody — and unrelenting sadness. Sadness often appeals to people — so does joy, and anger, but it is easier to relate to sadness no matter what age you are.

Now comes the return to "me-ness" since these are memoirs and not about anyone else, just this composer of a certain age and her experiences in writing, etc.

One of the commissions I liked most was to write a piano trio (piano, violin, cello), that would take up one-half of a concert program, so a work not much less than a half-hour in length.

If you like to compose you can go on "forever" making up ideas and developing them. So my one-movement trio evolved, unreeled for c. 28 minutes and was mostly written at the computer. It has a main theme and several sections that change in mood and even somewhat in style throughout its course. It was premiered at Frostburg State University (pianist Joan DeVee Dixon was the commissioner, by the way) and, believe it or not, the audience stayed awake — enthralled? — for the whole piece. *To wonder what is coming next* — isn't that what the essence of a piece of music should be, for the listener?

My *one*-movement concertos (piano, organ, marimba) are fairly lengthy, the piano concerto being the longest, and at its Kennedy Center performance it was deemed long-winded by some critic. After the performance a tall listener said to me "of course you'll have to shorten it". Did anyone ever say that to — hmmm — Mahler? Wagner? Of course not: the gods of music should not be questioned. (Emma Lou, dear, put back your daggers please; there is no cause for envy or malice in writing about music.)

And then there are the myriad organ pieces and piano pieces and songs that are only a few pages. Dale Wood, who asked me to write a number of collections of organ hymn settings recommended three pages, a certain number of measures, and he confessed that he himself put in repeats sometimes to achieve the proper length for publication purposes. (And after all, in a church service no one is going to sit quietly still for a long Offertory — folks become restless: dinner to cook, games to watch). Short pieces are a delightful challenge to write so I had no trouble with Dale's instruction.

Here's what I think: a composer (or a writer of short stories as well as novels) should be able to write a viable, entertaining prelude only a page in length as well as a "novel"-length concerto. The secret is to make either work so riveting that the listener will be happy to stay awake and interested throughout. That is the secret...how one does it! Maybe it's the *Quality....*

**The Flentrop Organ at the University of California Santa Barbara
in Lotte Lehmann Concert Hall**

Organ Music and Organists

Big names in keyboard music. Legends we have seen/ heard. *Rubinstein. Horowitz. Virgil Fox.* I heard Mr. Fox at a church in Washington, D.C. — I can't think of the name of the church, but it had a large choir loft in which we sat and could see the console and the organist.

I was with Helen Porter, a choral teacher at Swanson Junior High School in Arlington (I wrote the SSA "Alleluia" for her). Helen was a rather tall, pale, sweet woman with very curly hair — I have a niece who has hair like that, so beautiful. When Helen and I heard Virgil Fox, Helen had on a bright red hat. At one point near the beginning of his recital Fox looked at Helen and gave her a friendly, approving look. I still remember it, although I don't remember what he played — probably the Bach *T&F in D Minor.*

And about the same time I heard *E. Power Biggs* (Edward George Power Biggs) at, I believe, St. George's Episcopal Church in Arlington.

So I've heard two of the greatest organists in history.

Also two of the greatest contemporary artists: pianist *Yuja Wang* (33) and organist *Cameron Carpenter* (39).

Tremendous virtuosos, showpeople.

At UCSB (University of California, Santa Barbara) in Lotte Lehmann Concert Hall is a two-manual, 18-rank (that number sticks in my memory) Flentrop tracker action organ. It is a beautiful instrument and is hidden away on the right side of the hall and opened to view when a wall is slid to expose it.

The organ was installed in the early 70s and has an extremely light action — one could almost blow on the keys. A problem with some organists.

I heard *Gillian Weir,* the great British organist, give a recital on the Flentrop. She had absolutely no difficulty with the very light action. Her program included the Schoenberg *Variations on a Recitative.*

About 30 people attended Gillian Weir's recital, a disgraceful number, but typical of many organ recitals.

Gilliam Weir, Master Organist, whose career was noted by the *London Sunday Times* to be one of the 1000 Music Makers of the Millennium

I once gave one of the noontime Advent recitals at First Presbyterian in Santa Barbara, where I was organist, and there were nine people in the audience. It was almost the best playing that I had ever done, and I included a rather long improvisation (made it up on the spot — what else is an improvisation?) on *Paul Manz's* setting of the "Agincourt Hymn". (I sent him a tape of my improvisation and he graciously replied that he liked it.)

So the size of an audience is not always the most important factor in organ playing (though it's nice when a "good crowd" comes).

I wrote a piece for the Flentrop at UCSB. It was totally serial; it has a 12-tone row used in various ways. I constructed a row that expanded and contracted in pitch and a simple note-duration series. On the Flentrop the draw knobs can be partially pulled out and pushed in to change the stop's pitch and timbre. My pencil marks are probably still on the wooden draw knob stems.

Also, a slow ascending *glissando* in the middle section of the piece was easily played on the light-touch keyboard (a slow *glissando* is a bit difficult on most organs, the fingers or hand bumping along dangerously).

I remember that when I played this piece for the first time in a concert and started the *glissando* a man in the audience could be heard saying "there she goes".

Audience reactions: I read that in 18th century-19th century concerts audience members would sometimes exclaim enthusiastically *in the middle of a piece* if an especially lovely phrase or melody occurred!

James Welch played "Declarations" a few years ago on an anniversary concert for the Flentrop. A piece written for the Flentrop, performed on the Flentrop. Jim can play anything.

Sentimentality

After writing a bunch of music it's nice to write a bunch of prose. Maybe both are expendable, but who cares? Composers and writers keep on keeping on whether anyone is listening/reading or not. One is compelled.

Here is the topic: Sentimentality. When does that occur? Are some listeners enticed, some nauseated? It's a big concern of composers.

Sentimentality: "excessive tenderness, sadness, or nostalgia".

As I've said, it is some people's gag-producers; some people's bread of life. I've read that the Germans have a penchant for sentimentality. Too much brainwork? Too many fugues?

The Italians are extremely sentimental with all their opera arias.

The Spanish — give me a break. Russians, ditto. Etc.

Sentimentality in writing music often has to do with tonality, and chords coming from it. Tonality is one alternative to atonality. You can't be very sentimental about 12-tone pieces, a matrix, a diagram, or can you?

Oh, oh I've stepped on all the toes of post-tonality composers. I said in an earlier exposé that Milton Babbitt had tears in his eyes after a playing of one of his electronic pieces. Sentimentality? Alban Berg must have wept when writing his violin concerto, dedicated to Manon, the third child — dead at age 18 — of Alma Mahler, by Alma's second husband.

Incidentally, most pop music and most church service music very rarely has gone beyond tonality. So it's all sentimental?

No, it is "taste", knowing when to stop. Finding some musical solutions that are not too well-worn. Not looking for the easy way out. Mentality vs. sentimentality?

Too intellectual for me. I'll go write some more sometimes sentimental music.

DAYBREAK

For Mixed Chorus, S.A.T.B., and Piano

Text: John Donne

EMMA LOU DIEMER

N5597

Setting Poetry To Music

It is written that poetry and music developed side by side, the rhymes and rhythms and repetitions complementing each other, the music perpetuating the story or scene the poet is writing about. One enhances the other. It is possible to write music without words for inspiration, but certainly music inspired by poetry can have a "double whammy" (to put it unpoetically).

When I look for a poem to set to music, it must be one that creates an atmosphere in my consciousness, must "speak to me". When I set it to music, the poem becomes more meaningful, more vivid in its effect. And sometimes the beauty of the words is more important than the meaning.

I set to music Psalm 90. It was some years later than the setting of the Twenty-third Psalm written when I was c. 15 — a setting my siblings took comfort in singing following the death of our brother George. I put Psalm 90 to music for the choir when I was organist at Central Presbyterian Church in Kansas City (Missouri) in 1954.

Psalm 90 is a solemn psalm (try saying that quickly) and beyond my understanding. It is similar in form to some of the psalms that become rather violent and hopeless before there is a bit of redemption and resolution, some comfort at the end. Psalm 137 ("By the rivers of Babylon") is like that; I set that psalm for solo voice and piano while at Yale.

The beauty of the seventeenth century language of Psalm 90 in the King James Version of the Bible is there for all to read:

Psalm 90 (KJV)

Lord, thou hast been our dwelling place in all generations.

Before the mountains were brought forth, or ever thou hadst formed the earth and the world, even from everlasting to everlasting, thou art God.

Thou turnest man to destruction; and sayest, Return, ye children of men.

For a thousand years in thy sight are but as yesterday when it is past, and as a watch in the night.

Thou carriest them away as with a flood; they are as a sleep: in the morning they are like grass which groweth up.

In the morning it flourisheth, and groweth up; in the evening it is cut down, and withereth.

our years as a tale that is told.

Who knoweth the power of thine anger? even according to thy fear, so is thy wrath.

So teach us to number our days, that we may apply our hearts unto wisdom....

My setting is another piece of music that I can't find, but I remember that it was appropriately minor, dark in tone, and a bit troubled, moving. Rather Brahmsian.

Of course the praise psalms give us an excuse to write joyful, exalted music, and I've set quite a few of those, "O Come, Let Us Sing Unto The Lord" (Psalm 95) being one, written for the Arlington schools at a time when religious texts were historical rather than political. The music has a Stravinsky-like use of accented chords, and in places a Latin-ish rhythm, and repetitive patterns that Philip Glass would have been proud of. The piano part borders on "virtuosic". I guess it went out of favor when "praise music" with simpler concepts of style entered the scene in church music. But I still see it appearing sometimes on the web.

Love poetry is inspirational, like "Renouncement" by Alice Meynell, an early 20th century British poet:

> *I must not think of thee; and, tired yet strong,*
> *I shun the thought that lurks in all delight —*
> *   The thought of thee—and in the blue heaven's height,*
> *And in the sweetest passage of a song.*
> *Oh, just beyond the fairest thoughts that throng*
> *   This breast, the thought of thee waits hidden yet bright;*
> *But it must never, never come in sight;*
> *I must stop short of thee the whole day long.*
> *But when sleep comes to close each difficult day,*
> *   When night gives pause to the long watch I keep,*
> *And all my bonds I needs must loose apart,*
> *Must doff my will as raiment laid away, —*
> *   With the first dream that comes with the first sleep*
> *I run, I run, I am gathered to thy heart.*

(It's in my *Four Poems By Alice Meynell for Soprano or Tenor and Chamber Ensemble*.)

Or John Donne's "Daybreak":

> *Stay, O sweet and do not rise!*
> *The light that shines comes from thine eyes;*
> *The day breaks not: it is my heart,*
> *Because that you and I must part.*
> *Stay! or else my joys will die*
> *And perish in their infancy.*

I used that poem in *Madrigals Three* (not *Three Madrigals*), and I've discovered that young people sometimes seem to prefer melancholy lyrics to the "upbeat" ones.

I've set a lot of my sister's poetry to music (Dorothy Diemer Hendry — you can find her at dorothydiemerhendrypoet.com), mostly for solo voice. One of my favorites, written when she was 20, a nostalgic poem — but there is that hopefulness at the end, like a psalm:

Sonnet 25

All things that I have loved — where are they now?
A few have lingered in my sight and hearing:
My sister's hands, this flute, that apple bough,
Those hummingbirds are beauties still endearing.
And others charm my more reflective mind:
A bit of art, a line of verse, a motto,
A smell of pines, a draught of salt sea wind,
A heron's call, a cello's deep vibrato.
But how shall I account for lovely things
Too long since past for sight or memories,
White ships that bore me fast with love's great wings —
Are they now derelicts of midnight seas?
O fool! Though of my sight and mind small part,
All beauties past have havened in my heart.

And there are very familiar verses that are challenging to set like Emily Dickinson's "I'm Nobody":

I'm Nobody! Who are you?
Are you — Nobody — too?
Then there's a pair of us!
Don't tell! they'd advertise — you know!
How dreary — to be — - Somebody!
How public — like a Frog —
To tell one's name — the livelong June —
To an admiring Bog!

I included it in my *Seven Somewhat Silly Songs* song cycle.

And lighter poets like Ogden Nash:

"I don't mind eels
Except as meals
And the way they feels"

or
> *Celery, raw,*
> *develops the jaw,*
> *but celery, stewed,*
> *is more quietly ch*ewed.

I set some of the Nash verses for a high school boys' chorus in Arlington, and the boys didn't get the humor and felt insulted. Oh, well....

Toccata by Aram Khachaturian

S omeone mentioned how important the music (in this case piano music) of the "great masters" is. How important to read their immortal notes. By the "great masters" one usually means *Bach* and *Beethoven* and maybe *Brahms*, and perhaps *Mozart, Haydn*. From the sheer volume of works by them they are indeed great. Any of us who has "studied" piano, "taken" piano, and done it "seriously", has played a lot of their music.

I recently gave away most of my piano music, accumulated over many, many years, some of it more or less priceless including the mealy-material copies on which some of the editions of the Debussy preludes were printed. But I kept a few works, one of which will surprise the lovers of the "great masters". It is:

Toccata by *Aram Khachaturian!*

You'll say what? why? He's not a "great master", his music is rather light-weight, he probably didn't write many fugues or canons. Hmmmmm.

I don't remember where or why I bought this piece. It was published in 1945. In my teenage years of piano-playing I sometimes hurried down to Burchfield's Music Store in Warrensburg where I could find piano music; I may have discovered it there. Or perhaps it was at Jenkins Music Store in Kansas City where the bright orange cover of the toccata caught my eye (covers are very important).

For years I had dutifully played, learned a lot of the "great masters" and pieces that piano teachers gave me, pieces they had learned. Sorry folks, but Mozart and Haydn didn't "turn me on" in those years. (Nor did Bach until I heard a pianist at Yale play it with — feeling! Something besides mechanics — revelation!).

Khachaturian's *Toccata* did stir my pianistic impulses. It had dynamic contrasts, rhythmic drive, a timbre-conscious use of the piano, textural color, a wavering toward B minor but never quite there. I'm afraid Mozart paled by comparison. And I was off! Prokofiev came later, a much more difficult and diverse composer. But for my teenage sensibility Khachaturian was it, and I still love that piece.

I even wrote a difficult work, later, for violin and piano titled "Catch-A-Turian-Toccata" — Phil Ficsor and I performed it. (It was written for another duo, and that someone else wasn't wild about it. And it's a very wild piece. Wilder than Khachaturian).

Why do I improvise these days? To create something new, *without the notes*. Some pianists who are fine note-readers (as I was, am) do not know how to improvise. There are lessons on the web, or there are in-person teachers. There are many styles; some of us have our own, and it is constantly changing.

What have I played over the decades, from the *notes?* Music by these composers: Bach, Beethoven, Brahms, Mozart, Haydn, Domenico Scarlatti (one of my favorites), Chopin, Liszt (some), the Schumanns (Robert & Clara), Schubert, Debussy (all the Preludes), Ravel (Tombeau, Sonatine), Albeniz, Granados, Mussorgsky, Schoenberg, Hindemith, Bartok (above all), Gershwin, Prokofiev, Shostakovich, Scriabin, Poulenc, Satie, Scott Joplin and other ragtimers, Keith Jarrett, Dave Brubeck, L. Bernstein, Norman Dello Joio, Aaron Copland, Grazyna Bacewicz, Judith Zaimont, Barbara Pentland, and many, many others.

(It's too bad that some composers who specialize in opera-writing do not write piano music as a rule.)

And everyone should take time to improvise. Sometimes it's more fun than *reading the notes* of the "great masters".......

for Marjorie and Wendell Nelson

VARIATIONS FOR PIANO, FOUR HANDS
"Homage to Ravel, Schoenberg, and May Aufderheide"

EMMA LOU DIEMER

do not synchronize hands
resonant, legato, non-metric

continue pattern

*much pedal
(enter ad lib)

continue previous patterns ad lib

*The pedal may be changed occasionally, but the notes must run together, blur.

Writing Away from the Keyboard

For the first few decades of composing I sat at a keyboard of some sort, usually the piano, to write music, improvising until some idea seemed worth writing down.

I still do that often, playing through the whole "piece", getting a very rough idea of how to progress, what the outline might be.

If it's a choral work, I do somewhat the same thing, looking at the poem, the stanzas, the words, and making notations in the text about what should happen in the music: "tonality of...", "build up...", "contrast...", "repeat A...", etc.

And then sometimes, for a choral work or song, I write out a melodic line, often for the whole piece, and then go back and fill in the harmonies, the counterpoint (and of course move the main melodic line around so that it isn't always on top).

If it's an instrumental work, I sketch out the harmonies and sections. This was especially true when writing "Variations for Piano Four Hands — Homage to Ravel, Schoenberg and May Aufderheide" where the work is based on a 12-chord series, each section a different textural variation on the chord series).

When writing at the computer, I do it "all at once", from measure to measure, "thinking up" the ideas, patterns, rhythms, and inserting it all with the poor over-worked mouse.

The problem with writing at the computer, if it's a keyboard piece, is that I have to learn to play it. It was/is much more satisfying to write at a piano and have it in the fingers from the beginning.

But I tend to wander away in improvising and lose most of what I've played (unless I'm recording into a notation program on the computer while playing into it from an attached keyboard.)

The most fun is to write out the piece in pencil, the "old-fashioned" way, and then put it into the computer and see it beautifully reproduced, but that is time-consuming. I think many composers write at the computer, from songs to orchestral scores.

So for the first many decades of composing I wrote at the piano, before there was any computer music notation, and that was before (for me) 1985.

I wrote a few pieces away from any keyboard instrument. I would sit in the patio outside my house, in the spring or summer air, and compose the work and write it down with pencil on manuscript paper.

One work I wrote that way was "Pianoharpsichordorgan"—as you might guess, for those three instruments. It used some graphic notation — chord clusters, wavy lines — but mostly actual notes, no bar lines, or dotted barlines that indicated phrases or sections instead of a regular meter.

This will sound amateurish to a composer who has only used graphic notation, charts, diagrams, various symbols, drawings. But what I did was fairly new to me.

That piece, composed sitting outside on the patio, was played at UCSB by pianist John Clark, organist James Welch, and harpsichordist (me). We wore headphones to coordinate with each other and had a memorable seven-minute time, following the open score so we could see what everyone was playing.

Another work written away from a keyboard was the flute, oboe, harpsichord and tape piece for Bernie Atkinson, Clayton Wilson, and myself. One section had each instrument playing with a pre-recorded recording on their instrument. The last section was the instruments and tape altogether. An amusing part (at least the audience laughed) was when the harpsichord tape had loud clusters and I wasn't doing anything. Mild humor.

Other composers have done far more elaborate creations, set-ups, staging, sound production and manipulation. But I'm primarily a rather traditional composer and don't like too much clutter, too much complication, too much distraction from the musical sounds themselves. Just play the music, please.

SECTION EIGHT
Not Necessarily About Music

(Top) Emma Lou Diemer with her dog Mickey by the Lily Pond at Selmo Park; (Below) ELD's sister Dorothy and husband Wick certainly admired the Lily Pond at Selmo Park with their own representation of the old pool at their own house in Huntsville, Alabama

The Lily Pool

My niece, Betty, reminded me that when I wrote about our house in Warrensburg, I forgot to mention the lily pool! My mother had it filled in when families with children started living in faculty housing behind "our" property that included the pool. But before that it was a joy. It was rectangular and fairly large, and held lily pads and lilies including lotuses that bloomed periodically. It also had frogs that sang at night and had offspring of tadpoles that my childhood friends and I liked to watch and place in glass jars, and we were filled with wonder that these wiggly beings would grow up to be frogs that sang (well, croaked).

My sister and brother-in-law and family in Huntsville, Alabama had a fish pond that I helped clean out occasionally when I visited. We slipped and slid down the sides and emptied out the fish into a tank. (My sister would write "don't you want to come and help us clean out the fish pond?"...but getting back to the one that we had in Warrensburg.

No one got into it except once my brother John waded in and retrieved a pistol of his that my mother had, with fury, thrown in. There were of course many goldfish in the pool, and we followed their progress for some years. The grassy area in front of the pool was a gathering place for receptions and for dogs to roll and children to play. (Of course we were very careful to not let them fall into the pool, and no one ever did.)

On the premises were also turtles, including a snapping turtle that once our cocker spaniel got hold of and discovered was not a toy.

A friend of my sister, a totally handsome man, a student at the college, helped me (I was nine) find turtles and toads some warm summer days (there is nothing like a summer day in Missouri *before* it gets too hot, or even then).

His name was Joe Smith, and his father had a shoe repair shop in town and his mother, Pearl, was one of my mother's best friends. I've always wondered about the life of Joe. After college he joined the FBI, but I know nothing beyond that. How many, many people come into our lives and then fade away during the years!

Something else I remember about living in that house: the moon that shone into my room and the smell of honeysuckle coming from the field to the south and the creaking of the boards at night as the old house settled. Good grief! I'll stop before it all sounds like "The Waltons"!!

Rowing in Eden

One of the many poems by Emily Dickinson that has inspired choral composers and poetry lovers over the years is "Wild Nights! Wild Nights!". I was one of the "inspired" composers, and I gave it of course an active piano part, the piano probably taking the part of the sea — restless and churning and a bit "wild".

I hadn't read any analysis of the poem until just now — why read someone's analysis? Just enjoy the poem! But I did look up "Rowing in Eden" (from her poem "Wild Nights! Wild Nights!") to make sure Dickinson was being literal rather than allusive. But read it and decide for yourself. It is a love poem.

Now the story: My friend Marilyn Skiöld moved to Santa Barbara some years ago. One of her daughters, Lisa, had already preceded her and had become a helicopter pilot in the US Army and eventually married a fellow pilot and bore two children. Another of Marilyn's daughters, Ann, was soon to come to the US and enroll at UCSB. Her other daughter, Mari, remained in Europe. Marilyn left behind a handsome, dashing Swedish husband — but that is another story she or one of her daughters will have to tell.

Marilyn is an adventurous person, in some ways a "blithe spirit", as her family and friends can attest.

In her first summer in Santa Barbara she swam in the ocean, explored the city and the mountains, driving sometimes along roads on the highest peaks in a little car (a yellow Fiat) that seemed to teeter on the edge of the abyss at times. When her mother visited, the looming, shadowy hills frightened her, but Marilyn with her particular brand of Scottish zest found them exciting.

One day I joined Marilyn on a trip into the mountains. We drove up San Marcos Pass, a winding road that can be treacherous if one is going too fast, especially descending, but which looks over the canyons to the sea as you ascend, and the islands beyond. It is a way to come to Solvang and the quaintness and deliciousness of that Danish town. Halfway to Solvang is Lake Cachuma, a Santa Barbara water source, and the lake varies in size depending on the amount of rainfall.

An aerial view of the west end of Lake Cachuma near Santa Barbara, California

On that day the lake seemed wide and inviting, and we rented a boat and took our lunch with us to have a picnic in the middle of the blue/gray expanse of water.

We rowed out to the middle of the lake, both of us good rowers, and had a bite to eat there in the quiet, occasionally sighting a mule deer on the banks or a hawk overhead.

After awhile we thought to return to the dock, the afternoon starting to darken a bit. But the wind had come up (or over or around or against us and the boat) and when we — either one of us, in turn — tried to row, we couldn't move, not an inch. The wind was too strong. We tried, labored, "pedal to the metal", and we wondered if we were destined to stay on that lake forever.

After some futile labor we heard a shout, and some distance away was a boat with several men in it. They had seen our struggles and were offering to help. Saved at last!

They came alongside and attached a line to the front of our vessel and began to tow us out of the wind and to the "shore".

What to give in return? During the tow we threw our bag of food to them, still enough to be a decent thanks offering.

I think of Emily's poem:

> *Wild nights - Wild nights!*
> *Were I with thee*
> *Wild nights should be*
> *Our luxury!*
> *Futile - the winds -*
> *To a Heart in port -*
> *Done with the Compass -*
> *Done with the Chart!*
> *Rowing in Eden -*
> *Ah - the Sea!*
> *Might I but moor - tonight -*
> *In thee!"*

"Rowing in Lake Cachuma" — it's nice to think about, in retrospect....

The Cleanliness of Keyboard Keys

This is about cleanliness, so it's apropos. In another story I mentioned the formidable Miss Schoen, who taught piano at the college in Warrensburg years ago and was aghast that I couldn't read music at age nine.

Miss Schoen cleaned the keys of the two pianos in her studio after *every* student. I can relate a bit to that, since I clean the keys of our Steinway every so often even though I'm usually the only one who plays it.

Once I was practicing for an organ recital at a church in Washington, D.C. and the console was below an open window. The keys were very dirty. Very dirty. I mentioned this to the church custodian and he brought a not very clean rag and cleaned the keys, though not very well, but better than before. That was the recital when putting on my organ shoes beforehand, I dropped them and the sound echoed through the church. One of my friends in attendance remarked to her neighbor "Emma Lou dropped her shoes!" — very observant, but kind of embarrassing.

That was a recital that received a good review from Paul Hume in the *Washington Post*. But that's another story for another time.

Also, at the church in D.C. where I was organist (Reformation Lutheran), a friend who worked at the Library of Congress came to practice sometimes and always left the keys dirty, maybe from all those books at the Library of Congress. (He was a rather well-known musician, so I won't mention names.)

Some church organs have terminally discolored keys because various organists through the years were not diligent in keeping them clean.

Cleanliness is next to you-know-what.

Earthquake

One summer afternoon Marilyn and I were reading the Sunday papers on the patio behind my house in Santa Antonio Village in Santa Barbara, California. It was August 13, 1978. Suddenly we were jolted and shaken and — in our deep wisdom — knew it was an earthquake. I could see the water heater jump in its footing and there were sounds of rattling, objects falling. Not being very brave, I ran to the gate and into the back yard. By contrast, Marilyn folded the paper she was reading and told me later that she thought that if it was the end of the world, there was not much she could do.

There were a few murmuring voices in neighboring duplexes, but other than that it was very quiet. We joined some neighbors who were standing on the grass and waited for whatever was to come next.

Apparently, the tectonic plates were satisfied for awhile and the shaking had stopped. So Marilyn and I ventured inside, wondering what we would find. My little harpsichord had tipped over and a small Korean figure had fallen over and broken but that was about all. We were lucky, that time — I suppose there will be worse quakes, the price of living in California.

We learned later that the quake, "only" a 5.2 magnitude, originated off the coast near the university and there was 15 million dollars damage there, some minor injuries. Over half a million books fell off the shelves in the library.

There happened to be an applicant for the music theory position staying at the house; she was away hiking in the hills at the time, but that was her introduction to the area. That night the aftershocks and the periodic creaking of the boards in the house kept me awake, and for some nights afterward.

There was a much more serious earthquake in 1925 with quite a bit of destruction in downtown Santa Barbara and 13 people killed. One result was the rebuilding of many structures in a Spanish style in the city and a new, very beautiful courthouse.

Scary at it was, I remembered with greater fright the tornados in Missouri. Once, when my mother and grandmother and I were living in the house in southeast Kansas City, and my sister and family next door, the news warned of a tornado coming in our direction. We hurried down to the basement (although my sister said her children stayed in their kitchen and made sandwiches in preparation for whatever adventure was to come!). The tornado passed a few miles away and destroyed a school and some lives. There are many such incidents in Alabama and other states in "tornado alley".

Another time, a few years later, very early in the morning my house in Santa Barbara began to shake. In those days we were told to stand in a doorway (now we are advised to station ourselves by a heavy object — like the piano?). So I stood in a doorway and waited. When the shaking stopped, my collie dog and I went outside and watched the morning light appearing, and again, there was the silence....

Fires

And then there are the fires. There are so many. They are given names according to where they originate: Romero Canyon, Painted Cave, Tea House, Jesuita, Thomas.

I had moved to a house on the West side of Santa Barbara and had a good view of the sweep of mountain range above the city. One summer, sitting on the front deck, I could see three separate fires burning in the foothills. Sometimes the ash from the various fires covered our property like snow.

There are a few that stand out especially in my memory. The Sycamore Canyon fire in July, 1977 was sweeping down toward the city itself before it was contained. I didn't have the television on and was playing the piano when a friend on the East Coast phoned to see if I was ok. That particular fire was the one that destroyed our flute professor's home, his flutes, and the Bösendorfer piano. That piano had either 92 or 97 keys — I've forgotten the number, just that it was more than 88.

Another was the Painted Cave fire in June, 1990 (I've looked up statistics because I don't have quite that degree of remembrance). We had readied a carrier for the cat and I had dragged down to the car a number of photo albums. I looked concernedly at our piano (as I did during every fire). Our neighbors were not leaving, Ron Weaver being a calm, reassuring man, so we stayed.

At around 10:00 p.m. the wind subsided and the fire was stopped near the foot of Modoc Road, not far away. In that fire people in my church lost their homes; our principal soprano, Audry Sharpe, lost her music library along with her home and escaped over the 101 just in time.

Another was the "Tea" fire in November, 2008, named for a structure above Montecito and Westmont College. The fire was apparently caused by young people (not from Westmont) who neglected to thoroughly put out a campfire they had started several hours earlier. The fire, fanned by 85-mile-an-hour Sundowner winds, heavily damaged buildings on the Westmont campus, and several hundred students and faculty sheltered in the gymnasium, a previously-designated safe structure, and were unharmed.

The Montecito Tea Fire (2008) — in Montecito and Santa Barbara

I had become acquainted with Philip Ficsor, violinist on the Westmont faculty, and he and I — at his instigation — had begun to rehearse and eventually record all my music for violin and piano.

In the Tea fire Phil and his family lost their home on the Westmont campus, although his studio where he had his violin was not burned. We rehearsed in a room at All

Saints Episcopal church in Montecito the morning after the tragedy — imagine doing that, the power, distraction of music, regardless....

The most recent was the catastrophic Thomas fire which began on December 4, 2017 near Thomas Aquinas College north of Santa Paula. Powered by Santa Ana winds, it was a firestorm, and swept through the Santa Ynez mountains and up the coast through Ventura and to Santa Barbara and was the largest wildfire, at the time, to have occurred in California.

In January the rains came and soon the mountain hillsides above Montecito erupted, broke away, and torrents of water and debris tore down into a large swath of the community. We, not far away in Santa Barbara, listened to the news and wept, knowing that — even though we were far away in all ways from the wealth and glamour of Montecito — places that we had frequented were in danger of being inundated. The flood rushed through homes, taking some residents with it, and the flow headed across 101 to the ocean. One little girl has never been found, one of 23 who perished. We can still drive by the destruction around the creek beds and nearby houses, in the process of being rebuilt.

Among the many photos was one of Oprah Winfrey, a Montecito resident, wading through the mud outside her home (on the estate she had bought for 50 million some years before).

Earthquake, fire, flood, and now pestilence. What a life we do lead....

Heights

Oh, dear, Barron Trump is taller than his father, who is 6'2 (or 6'3 depending on which story you're reading.) His mother is pretty tall. I have a fixation on height, being short. No one in my family was tall. My father was tallest at 10', about the height of Eisenhower and Truman, taller than Carter. I have a great nephew who is 6'8". Imagine being that tall!

Public figures I admire: Eleanor Roosevelt most of all, who was almost 6'. And Michelle Obama, ditto. However, another famous person I admire is Kamala Harris, who is only a little taller than I am.

Some people seem tall because of their bearing, their dignity, their intellect. I'm sure there are tall people who are quite stupid (and stoo-ped). In my family, most of the next generations are taller. In family photos I am astonishingly not tall, always a shock because I think of myself as rather tall.

The statistics show that many presidents have been tall. Wonder where that puts Franklin Delano Roosevelt who, though 6'2, was in a wheel chair most of his very public life (and also was, in my way of thinking, our greatest president after Abraham Lincoln, who was the tallest of them all. *Oh dear,* Barron Trump is taller — what will his future be, after his father is retired to Mar-a-Lago? Tallest man in the world?)

If some people *seem* taller because of their demeanor and intellect, no doubt the opposite is true: Very tall people can seem incredibly short because of their lack of grace, intellect, etc. It's a tall subject.

Joe Biden is fairly tall; he will tower over them all except for Kamala....

Easter Sunday 2020

Yesterday (Easter Sunday) was cloudy and a bit cool. Saturday had been sunny and gorgeous and of course we stayed home all day. But Sunday we took a drive, first to deliver/leave on a grassy area a few treats for a friend in a fairly nearby retirement community, Valle Verde. There are signs everywhere there to go, leave, do not enter. Such is the wise protection of the older residents. So we left the package and drove away quickly.

Then we drove through Hope Ranch, a suburb of Santa Barbara that has many large estates and horses (we saw only two). Part of it is hilly and all of it is beautiful. Several people were out walking in the road — there are no sidewalks — so we drove carefully. Everyone answered our waves — there is great camaraderie in times of stress.

We were looking for a place to take a walk, so we drove up Campanil Hill, way up where it seems as though the entire Pacific Ocean is spread out below. If I had five or ten million $$ or more I would like to live up there.

Then we drove past Hendry Beach where there were a number of cars, people getting take-out at the restaurant, and along Shoreline Park and Cabrillo to the wharf where State Street begins. Downtown shops and restaurants were mostly closed. Little traffic. One or two homeless, one a man with his two dogs.

State Street runs all the way through downtown and eventually winds up at the 101 Freeway, a long highway that stretches all the way from L.A. to Olympia, Washington.

There used to be a stoplight at the wharf, almost the only one between L.A. and San Francisco on the 101. Drivers would sit there for some minutes waiting for the light to change. It was finally taken away by popular demand.

We drove up State Street only to Micheltorena where Trinity Episcopal Church stands; it is the only example of Gothic architecture in a large swath of California. I could talk about Trinity and its pipe organ for some time. (It is one of some nine pipe organs in the SB area, the largest being at First Presbyterian, and perhaps the most interesting, a theatre organ, at the Arlington Theatre).

From Micheltorena to the West Side and home to watch the amazing, frightening, some faintly amusing programs on television.

It was a different Easter Sunday.

Up Early During the Pandemic

I awakened at three this morning. I don't know why. There was no noise that I remember — it would have to be a loud one for me to hear it.

We put out leftover food last night, in back, probably for the opossum who comes around. He or she lives someplace up in the hill with their family. They are quiet, beneficial animals, and neat. The raccoons that used to come at night were more raucous, knocked the food dish around, but cute — their faces!

Yesterday we went out to the university, stopping first at the bank, where distancing was being supervised by a guard, and then by the post office where I mailed the checks for my taxes.

The campus at the university was deserted, devoid of its 26,000+ students who for awhile will continue their education elsewhere. The parking lot by the music building had one car in it, and ours made two.

We walked over to the plaza below the bell tower where a 61-bell carillon is housed. Storke Tower is 190 feet tall, the tallest structure in the southern part of Santa Barbara County. I wrote a piece for the 50th anniversary of the carillon last year. The sounds of those bells are the first I noticed when I arrived on campus years ago. The tune that the carillon plays on the hour is constructed from the UC motto *Fiat lux* ("Let there be light"), using the number of letters in each word: 3-5-2-5, the numbers corresponding loosely to pitches (bells) on the carillon.

I wondered if the bells were working, if the setup was intact, and sure enough we heard the tune and the low C sound four times correctly for four o'clock.

Storke Tower and the Carillon Bells on the campus of UCSB

Later (maybe in the early hours this morning) I thought of Leonard Cohen's lyric:

> *Ring the bells that still can ring*
> *Forget your perfect offering*
> *There is a crack in everything*
> *That's how the light gets in*

Glimpses

I lie awake sometimes thinking of all the famous people I've never seen or will ever see. (Not really — I'm happy to see some lovely, though not world-famous, people quite regularly.)

But I lived in the Washington, D.C. area for 12 years and never saw a president — although I believe I had a glimpse of President Lyndon Johnson once at Arlington Cemetery. The president was looking out from his limousine, a sad face on a sad day. I had a glimpse of Ethyl Kennedy at a horse show, but no other Kennedys or any other of our famous leaders.

And in Santa Barbara I have no knack for spotting celebrities. My friend Marilyn is more observant and had glimpses in past years of Robert Mitchum, and Vincent Price, in Montecito, and Charlton Heston coming out of Macy's one day. She said he gave an adoring little boy a ride around the parking lot in his limo.

And she thought she saw Oprah Winfrey driving a car in Montecito one day. (We don't live in Montecito but like to go there sometimes to a favorite lunch place — Montecito Coffee Shop — known as "the pharmacy", open for take-out now, I believe).

I have spotted our city mayors now and then. Most of them have been women for the last 40 years. Harriet Miller endeared herself to me because I noticed her chewing gum at a music concert at the Unitarian Society once. (She was an excellent mayor). And I believe it was Mayor Marty

Blum who tried to get into our Prius by mistake one day
— it was exactly like her own car.

But my biggest glimpse — longer than a glimpse —
happened one Easter Sunday at the church where I was
organist: First Presbyterian. I had played the Prelude and
had the first hymn up ready to play after announcements.
Then there was a commotion among the congregants and
everyone stood up and began clapping. I looked where
everyone was looking and saw Nancy and Ronald Reagan
coming down the aisle. It is surreal to see "in the flesh"
extremely familiar people one has viewed innumerable
times in photos, even in the movies. *I stood up on the organ
pedals to see them.* (Fortunately, I had canceled all the stops.)

We all stared in astonishment — Reverence? Pride? —
as the Reagans sat down in the corner of a front pew. Then
our minister, Bob Pryor, spoke a welcome to them and the
service continued.

I remember that for the organ Offertory I played (my)
rousing setting of "Llanfair," one of the tunes to *Christ the
Lord Is Risen Today!* in which at one point the melody is in
the booming pedal. Not your usual quiet Offertory.

After the service we all rushed to the side doors to see
the Reagans drive off, probably to their ranch above Santa
Barbara.

They never visited our church again. (I wonder if it was
because of the loud organ Offertory?)

The Mystical Number Eleven

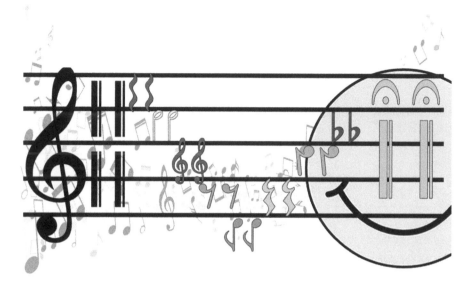

This is a "shorty" and doesn't have anything to do with music. On second thought, it does, in a way. One of the movements of *By the Sea* for piano four hands that I very recently wrote for Tachell Gerbert ad Bradley Gregory is in 11/8 meter all the way through.

This "shorty" is about the number *Eleven*. Here are the facts:

I was born on Thanksgiving Day, November 24 (you can look up the year).

November is the *Eleventh* month.

I was born in our house in Kansas City, Missouri at 6511 Edgevale Road.

6 plus 5 equals *Eleven*.

And *Eleven* is *Eleven*.

(The house is still there—no plaque, but in good shape.)

My father was born on December *Eleven*.

My mother was born *Eleven* years before the end of the 19th century.

(She always said you could add *Eleven* to any year and you'd have her age.)

My grandmother was born in 1867. If you add those numbers together you get 22, half of which is *Eleven*.

My sister Dorothy was born on April *Eleven*.

My twin brothers, George and John, were born on June *Eleven*.

In Kansas City the house that we lived in after the one on Edgevale Road was 443 W. 57th Terrace. 4+4+3 equals *Eleven*.

When we moved from Warrensburg back to Kansas City, after my father retired, our house was at seventy-three *Eleven* Manchester.

My sister's house in Huntsville, Alabama was at 2603...add those and you get *Eleven*.

My office number at UCSB was 1111. *Eleven Eleven*.

However, that is the extent of the California/*Eleven* connection.

I guess my heart is in Missouri.

There is nothing like trivia. But I have been waiting to tell this to someone. Maybe you have strange coincidences in your family.

My family, as my friend Marilyn would say, is *Weird!*

Do You Pray?

Do you pray? I know that's a private matter for some. Most of us do — pray. Some do it at prescribed times during the day and night, periodically, organized, disciplined.

Some do not pray. To whom do agnostics and atheists give thanks or render supplication, ask for help? Not my business. We are not to be judgmental. Do not cast the first stone, etc.

Of course I grew up in a family that said "grace" before every meal when we were together. I had a little prayer that I was taught as a child and that I mumbled quickly (Father of all in heaven above, we thank thee for thy love, our home and food and all we wear show thy loving care. Amen) when my mother assigned me at mealtime (I dreading having to speak, being annoyingly shy and uncommunicative in that regard).

Prayer. I can remember going to lunch at a nice tea room at Brookside in Kansas City (Missouri) with my mother and seeing her in that public place bow her head before our meal. And at my sister and brother-in-law's house, my brother's, too, we all held hands and heard thanks given.

At going-to-sleep time I sometimes remember to pray. It is a calming, purposeful train of thought. However, during the silent attempt of running through the prayer about the fourteen angels, the Lord's Prayer, the Twenty-Third Psalm, all the many relatives and close friends — all I can bring to mind, our country, maybe the world (although that is hard to wrap one's cognizance about)...during all that my mind has usually wandered to the next day's activities or the music, always the music, that is playing in my brain — during all that, the prayers have become lost (in thought).

Some people pray all the time: we pray that we do not fall or fail or forget. Thank Heaven for prayer.

We Gather Together

I awoke this morning at 3. I don't know why. There was no earthquake, no fire. But there was the sight of those hundreds of people on the bridge; I wondered if the bridge would hold or would break apart. And the rot in the White House (this was written before Biden's election). The rot in the Senate (same but still here). The rot in the Supreme Court (ditto). The "Trump first family" doing their best to break apart the country — as long as their investments are okay. In 2020 it was all about Trump (in the absent minds of his loyal followers).

And there is my family. Love. For the dear one down the hall — her family almost as well-known to me as my own. My family. Six generations that I know: my grandmother, my parents, my siblings, their children, their children's children, etc. Six generations. The latest: Emerson Augsburger; Aria Rose Velasquez.

It is strange to be the oldest of them all. It is usually the young writers who write about the old ones. I would like to write about each family member — but some of them must do that. There should be a writer in every family, to write about the old ones and the young ones.

And there is this beautiful day. And music. And the birds. And the sky.

We will not break apart.

SECTION SEVEN
Animals and Cars I Have Known

My special friend, Dewdrop, enjoying time with me outside his cage in the 1950s

Dewdrop

It's so gratifying to hear about other people's experiences with their cats and dogs that they cherish or cherished. Do indulge me for telling about Dewdrop.

One early morning, at the house in southeast Kansas City in which my mother (and my grandmother and I) lived after my father retired from the college in Warrensburg (and died soon after) we looked out into a little garden area where there were roses and saw a small, young blue parakeet perched on a branch. He was no doubt someone's pet that had flown away from his home.

Of course we took him inside and hurried to get a cage and food for him. And we put a notice in the local paper in the lost-pet column — fortunately to no avail. He was ours, and we named him Dewdrop because he came to us in the early morning dew. (Clever, huh?)

We trained him soon to jump on our finger in the cage and to eat bird seed and sip water from a dish. (All his life we never gave him anything but bird seed except for an occasional nibble of lettuce or apple. I had a friend once who gave her parakeet lots of things including sherry and the poor bird didn't live very long).

Dewdrop began to talk quite soon, repeating names and phrases my nieces and nephew (who lived next door) taught him. Sometimes when he thought no one was listening, no one to distract him, he strung together all the phrases and sentences he knew, getting them out in a kind of *sotto voce* voice that you wouldn't think to interrupt. He knew quite a bit and went on for some time, talking to himself.

When we felt secure in letting him out of the cage to fly around and perch on our hands or some object, he found that my mother's shoulder was a good place to sit, and while she was reading the newspaper or eating an apple he felt free to join in those activities.

For detail a parakeet that looks much like Dewdrop

At night, to be sure he didn't fly away, my mother held him securely in her hand while she went around the house closing the curtains and making sure the doors were locked before she put him in his cage. Some people have a way with little pets, and little children — she did.

At one time we decided he must be lonesome and we got him a green, lady parakeet and put her in his cage. He was fine with having her as company, but she was very unsettled and flopped around and made such a fuss we feared for his safety. Back to the pet shop she went, and Dewdrop was an only bird again.

Sometimes, when he was feeling under the weather, he would rest his head on my finger. Have you had a bird that did that?

During those later years I was going to school at Eastman and then living in Virginia in the winters, returning home in the summers, and after my mother died there were two things I took back East: the piano and Dewdrop.

And when I moved to California, the car held two dogs, a cat, and Dewdrop. He lived in his cage at my place up on Miramonte Drive in Santa Barbara and passed his last year or two there. He was twelve years old.

Some people don't like pet birds, and I must admit that it is not nice to have a caged anything when you assume they might rather be free. But people being people, some of us like to have beautiful things, watch them, listen to them, teach them tricks, care for them.

And Dewdrop came to us, after all....

**(Top) Our Tippy and Tuffy were like sisters, often sleeping together
(Below) Tippy and I enjoying the neighborhood together**

Cats and Dogs

This is about cats and dogs, so if you don't like pets, don't bother to read it. It does, however, have a little about music, which is the topic of most of the other stories.

When we moved to Warrensburg from Kansas City, we didn't bring a pet with us, or even have one at that time, although we did earlier and also a duck. But in Warrensburg we seemed to have inherited the dog that belonged to Dr. Hendricks, the outgoing president of the college (CMSTC at that time, now University of Central Missouri) whose place my father was taking, along with the house (Selmo Park, which is no longer in existence).

The dog was a lively ginger-colored cocker spaniel who liked to chase and bark at cars, and he was soon hit by one. There was a long driveway in a wide, oblong circle around the house starting and ending at South Holden Street. Delivery and mail trucks coming around the house were invitations for lively, barking dogs.

Since we needed a dog in the family, we acquired another cocker spaniel, a black one that we named Mickey. He liked to listen to the piano and would lie next to the pedals, practically under my feet, when I played. (And if I played too loudly, he would howl.)

Mickey was a sweet and rambunctious pet. He lasted about two years before he, too, was killed by a car either in the driveway or on the street.

I remember that my mother hated to tell me of the loss of Mickey and was grateful that I took it so well. She knew that a dog was necessary; I think it is necessary for many, perhaps most children — and adults?

After Mickey there were two or three other dogs, one of which I encouraged to follow me home but that was later claimed by the owner. And a cute, spirited collie-type that I named Rocky, for Rachmaninoff. We were afraid he would meet the same fate as the two cocker spaniels so we gave him to some friends in the country.

We also had a few kittens from the college farm that were taken away from their mother too soon, and a larger cat that mistook my mother's bed for a litter box and was given away.

But it was necessary to have a dog.

My mother and I went to Kansas City and got two English shepherd puppies that I named Lancelot and Elaine. Unfortunately, they both developed a serious skin infection — mange? I can remember bathing them and sobbing at their ailment that I couldn't cure and that we couldn't keep them.

Once again my mother saved the situation and we took the two puppies back and chose another one. She was tiny and not too well when we brought her home and I can remember my grandmother holding her in her hand and probably willing her to be all right. And she was, and lived with us twelve years. I named her Jolie because she was so pretty.

Jolie lived a charmed life. She grew to be a mid-size, healthy, beautiful pet, and although she barked at trucks, especially postman-types, and sometimes chased them, she was never hit. She padded over to the college campus where she had become acquainted with two of the women teachers and would spend several hours in one of their offices before coming back home. In other words, she walked safely from our house, down to South Holden Street, up Union Street to the campus and then through the quadrangle to her friends' offices. Sometimes she stopped in at our father's office and stayed awhile. All of this with nary a mishap. Jolie was an amazing dog.

She was afraid of thunderstorms and would bark ferociously at the thunder — and of course fireworks were a torment, as to most dogs.

When we moved back to Kansas City upon my father's retirement, she was still with us in the new home. One strange habit she had was, when her food dish was put down, she would run rather hysterically out into the yard barking away any imaginary neighbor dog that might want her dinner. Jolie was a member of the family for — as I've said — 12 years.

Many years later, in Santa Barbara, I had at first three Pekingese dogs and a white Persian cat and after their departure a collie dog named Tippy and a part-Persian cat named Tuffy. They came at the same time and grew up

Tuffy keeping me company while I compose on my electronic keyboard

together. The cat was unusual because she liked the sound of any electronic instrument but hated the piano. When I would start to play, she would let out a cat distress cry and run for the door. I figured out finally that she liked to lie on the piano strings and when someone played, it disturbed her rest.

Tuffy, like Jolie, led a charmed life. We had coyotes in the area at night and they were a danger to little animals. Small and furry Tuffy liked to lie out in the driveway after dark and couldn't be persuaded to come in until late. She was never bothered. We wondered if it was because big dog Tippy was well-known in the vicinity.

One day we came home and were amazed and frightened to see Tuffy walking around on the deck railing with a coyote after her. However, Tippy was on the deck and barking at the coyote who soon jumped to the ground leaving Tuffy safe and sound with her protector, Tippy.

After 12 years Tippy, as is the case with many larger dogs, had trouble walking and we had begun to have to lift her up the stairs and noticed her increasing loss of general strength. Tuffy watched, noticed all this, and shortly after Tippy died, Tuffy did too.

There is one last experience with Tippy — that beautiful, proud, smart collie dog — that I'll always remember. The night before we were to take her to her veterinarian doctor to put an end to her suffering, she came, crawled really, to me and looked at me with those searching eyes that I imagined saying "it is time".

Don't tell me cats and dogs don't have souls....

**(Top) My part-Persian kitty, Tuffy
(Below) My Collie Tippy**

Tippy and I watching a neighborhood ballgame on one of our leisurely but memorable walks while she was in the family

Old Dogs

This is a little bit political, so best to go back to tending your house plants or working on a new recipe for dinner — or, in my case, writing a calming piece of music.

It has to do with an item that appeared in one of the news sources recently. I took it personally, and rather than referring to the publication or the "critic", I'll express an opinion on the topic.

One does not disparage another's beloved pets — dogs, any animal one holds dear. We had a big dog, a collie named Tippy. She was a beautiful, proud member of the family and an excellent watch dog.

As Tippy grew older she, on our walks, sought the shade and liked to lie down in the cool grass. When she was twelve, we needed to help her climb the many steps up to our front door. Finally, it was too much for all of us and we, humanely, had to let her go.

But if anyone had criticized her or cast any kind of aspersion on our beautiful aging dog I would have gladly pushed, in my mind's eye, that person down those seventeen steps. Bumpity, bumpity, bumpity. All the way down to the concrete slab at the bottom.

Theo, our neighbor's cat in Santa Barbara who loves to come inside and talk about his day

Distractions

This rumination may seem frivolous at first, but never fear, it will change.

One of the distractions we have is the television commercials. I like the one of the woman who comes home after a hectic day at the office and finds her living room a hubbub, noisy — her husband clowning with the children, the dog barking, things flying through the air. The woman rolls her eyes and goes back to her car where she sighs, closes her eyes, and contentedly enjoys the peace and quiet.

Another is the big emu who squawks a lot and is playing in a volleyball game and at one point sees the ball coming toward him. It lands in front of him and he (she?) sits on it protectively.

I don't like the commercials with children eating spaghetti or women and men perspiring in the fitness room or medicines whose warning labels are longer than the benefits. But commercials are a distraction.

The outgoing president was at first faintly amusing with his misspelled words, his form of exercise parading at rallies clapping for himself, going around the table while members of his cabinet lauded him. But amusement began to turn to anger, then hatred, for his actions, too numerous to list. And lately, this week, anger has turned to fear — for ourselves and our country.

The most important person in the world is a strong woman of 80, mother of five. The Speaker of the House. She is not easily distracted.

Our neighbors' cat, Theo, comes to visit us. He stays a little while to be petted and talked to. But soon he becomes restless, watchful, wary, alert. And goes away to other duties and interests.

We should be wary, watchful, not distracted. It's not a make-believe world.

Theo has such big curious eyes and loves to hear the piano before trapsing off on another adventure

Cars

I've been discussing music topics throughout this "memoir," but wanted to write a little about *Cars!* And the fact that sometimes people give them names and make them part of the family.

The first family car that I remember was a Pierce Arrow with jump seats, room for our family of seven. Once my mother and father were driving in it and my father had to slam on the brakes before hitting some object and my mother ended up on the floor. My father said "I've ruined my *Car!*". My mother pretended never to forgive him for that.

(In those early days there were of course no seat belts, no reverse lights, no turn signals, etc.)

When we moved from Warrensburg back to Kansas City, we had a 1954 Buick Roadmaster, the first car I remember that had automatic windows.

My twin brothers, when they were in college, had a series of *Cars* they bought for a few dollars and brought home and worked on, in or outside our garage. (My father would groan a bit when they came up the driveway with yet another.)

However, there was not a bunch of cars parked outside, just one car at a time, being worked on.)

My brother John built a very small car that you could ride in. And he taught me to drive in a Model T Ford he had bought for ten dollars. John was a good teacher, and only laughed a little when I jerked and chugged along in the beginning. I was fourteen.

My brother George had bought a big Packard for a few dollars, and I stalled it on a hill once. He, too, was patient. (My mother told me once that she had to hire a man to teach her to drive because my father became too upset when she had difficulty with the clutch, etc.)

My brothers had one or two *Cords*, a snappy-looking sports car that looked better than a Porsche, neater than a Corvette.

We all drove except my grandmother. My father, who had really only one good eye — his left eye was a little clouded — drove at a moderate speed around Warrensburg, thinking of the college he was administering and not bothering to give a signal when he turned left. He never had an accident (Marilyn says there must have been cars piled up behind him.)

My mother was a good and moderate driver. She never had an accident, though once, when her eyesight was not perfect any more, she said she ended up in the middle of a snowy field in Southeast Kansas City where we lived. What bothered her most was when on a Sunday morning she would aim for a parking spot outside church and some "whipper snapper" would get there first. (Remember Kathy Bates in the movie where she gets even with some young "whipper snappers" in a similar situation?).

My sister was a good driver, and had a little blue convertible when she started teaching in a small town named Peculiar, in Missouri. Has anyone heard of that town?

My first car was a used 1952 blue Chevy. I traded it for a used 1957 pink Bel Air Chevrolet, that I've mentioned before, and drove it to Arlington, Virginia and back to Kansas City many times.

Finally, there was a new Chevy, an Impala, the same color as my house in Falls Church. And then a (used) white Oldsmobile convertible with red seats.

And after moving to California I admired a (used) green and white 240Z (Datsun at the time) in a showroom in Santa Barbara and bought it. On Sunday mornings I parked it in the organist's parking place at the Christian Science church where I was organist, and I think people wondered what kind of music I was going to play.

Then came a new 260Z and a series of Toyotas, a Mazda, and finally the hybrids — one of the first Prius(es) in Santa Barbara in 2001. Joan Rutkowski came to see it once, and I was flattered that she was interested in our car!

And now a Nissan Leaf that plugs into a charger in the garage and uses not a drop of gasoline.

Love cars, though I don't know a thing about them. Hope you enjoyed the music as much as I loved my *Cars!*

In the library in the Diemer residence in Kansas City (after GWD's
retirement from Central Missour State) in 1956. Grandfather George
Willis Diemer enthralls his grandchildren on the wonders of the world.

Pictured with George (L to R) are George Diemer III and brother
Jack, Bonny Hendry in grandpa's capable hands, Betty, Terri and Alan
Hendry, and near the globe René Deimer

FINALE
Those to Follow

Being one humble and rather aged writer I cannot possibly cover the vast array of generations, family members, who are present and who are younger, some very young. But a few words about them, for posterity, for future writers.

There were at least two births in the extended family last year (2020). And two more scheduled. I am lucky if I know everyone's name, let alone able to see them at my age and in this pandemic.

I haven't been to Huntsville, Alabama for several years to see some of the progeny of Dorothy and Wick. Nor have I been to Kansas and Philadelphia and Marlborough and Columbus and Baltimore to see the families of Lois and John. There is no help in me.

I love them all. Love grows in our families. It is always present.

In these stories I have not gone further than the family I grew up with. Little detours to beloved in-laws, but not to what would be the grandchildren of my parents.

And I have apologized at some point for the me-ness of the stories. My goal in the beginning was to write about my journey as a woman composer, nothing more. You see, women are often soon forgotten. Women composers even sooner. I protest.

But in writing about oneself and one's small career one soon remembers those who are closest to oneself — because they are related, by blood or by marriage.

(Top) The 80s Models, boy cousins all born in 1980, with their moms, Bonny and Scott, Terri and Sam, Betty and Chris; (Bottom) A large Diemer family reunion at Dorothy and Wick's home in 1992

And that is a wonderful thing: to have so many relations of one sort or another that there is no time to cover them all, or even begin. Those to follow must do that.

But I need to write a little about the children of Dorothy and Wick, and the children of Lois and John. There are four surviving offspring of Dorothy and Wick. The fifth, a baby boy, died at eight months. I remember Byron as an exquisitely beautiful baby, just born, and a few months later in Warrensburg gazing at me from his crib with his sister, Betty, nearby, also looking at me with those questioning eyes that babies seem to have.

Betty was the first of the new generation and a sweet, curly-haired child I carried around, being the adoring aunt. Imagine! She is tall and elegant now, an accomplished musician and mother of four children she and Larry Augsburger have given to the world. Theresa, Deanna, Brett, Chris.

And Terri, whose delightful sense of humor and intelligence matched that of her late husband, Dr. Richard Sims, and is there in their children. Julie, Sam, John.

And Alan, mysterious and independent and doing well working in Ohio. He phoned his mother frequently during her illness. She would stop whatever she was doing to talk with him.

And Bonny, now married to Steve Gierhart, and the mother of Dr. Scott Pfitzer. She is a book to be written, her love of horses and dogs, and her work as a program manager with NASA.

And the Diemers who Lois and John nurtured and tended. George III, delightful in his knowledge and curiosity and imagination and married to wonderful Paula.

And René, mother of five with Lutheran minister/administrator Philip Krey, and with a sharp intelligence and stability through all the years. And their children — Jessicah, Lindsay, Noah, Jordan, Micah.

And Jack (John Irving II), inventive and resourceful and profoundly verbal. And married to lovely Kay, who is exotic and extroverted — unlike the more reticent Diemers

— and who gave the world and Jack a talented daughter in Dr. Marilyn Diemer Velasquez.

And, lastly, but always unique, Dee Dee (Deidre) Diemer, author and people person with business acumen, and a budding ornithologist. Dear Dee Dee. She was six when her father, John, died.

As I have said, all these dear individuals and their children and the next children are a hundred times more worthy than I, to be written about and studied.

There is much variety and brilliance in our families. Do not let it go unnoticed.

And I thank one of those brilliant family members, Steven Gierhart, for editing and arranging for these stories to be made available. And Larry and Betty Augsburger and Bonny Gierhart for their expertise. And anyone else who cares to read about someone's examined life, a life mostly centered around music and its creation. "Life without music is no life at all...." or however that imagined song should go.

The Diemer family reunion in 1992 but with George and Myrtle's grown grandchildren; (L to R) top row George III and Jack Diemer, Alan Hendry, Dee Dee Diemer, and bottom row René Diemer Krey, Betty Hendry Augburger, Terri Hendry Sims, and Bonny Pfitzer-Gierhart

Other Images of
Family, Friends and Colleagues

(Left) ELD at two years old after a scolding

(Below) John, Dorothy, Emma Lou, George. c. 1928

Emma Lou the young teenager in 1941

(Left) Emma Lou enjoys the outdoors c 1945

(Right) Emma Lou readies for an event c 1956

(Above) Lizzie Casebolt in the library at Selmo Park. c. 1956

(Above) Myrtle, Emma Lou, George. 1953 on a vacation to Italy

(Top) ELD at Hendricks Hall in 1950 before a performance; (Right) Emma Lou as a young woman in 1950

(Top) ELD on a trip to Huntsville (c 1969) to visit family; (L to R-ELD, Niece Betty Augsburger and daughter Theresa, Niece Bonny and Betty's husband Larry; (Below) Another happy Christmas in Huntsville c 1967; (L to R-Sister Dorothy, Dorothy's children Alan, Bonny, Terry and ELD)

(Left) Emma Lou at National City Christian Church, Washington D.C. 1986

(Right and Below) at First Presbyterian in Santa Barbara in the 1990s

(Top) ELD Friend Ellen Schlegel. Author, Biographer

(Below-L to R) Dale Wood, ELD, and Lorenz reps

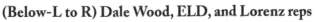

(Top) Members of
Santa Barbara AGO.
David Gell on right
and ELD in blue, 4th
from right

(Left) Friend Pauline
Oliveros at UCSB.
1985

(Top) Marilyn Skiöld, Betty Oberacker, Ann Skiöld

(Bottom) ELD, and friends Tod and Millie Fortner, Julie Neufeld.

(Top) Recording in Bratislava with Joel Suben and Nathan Daughtrey

(Bottom) ELD and Rev. Arnold Keller. c. 1982

(Top) Sisters Terri Sims and Bonny Pfitzer Gierhart with husband Steve visit Emmie and Marilyn in Santa Barbara in October 2009

(Bottom) Visit to Niece Bonny and Steve's farm in Huntsville in April 2005; (L to R- Emmie, Marilyn, Wick, Dorothy and Bonny)

About the Author

Emma Lou Diemer was born in Kansas City, Missouri on November 24, 1927.

Her parents were Myrtle Casebolt Diemer (1889-1961), homemaker and church worker. Her father was George Willis Diemer (1885-1956), educator, college president. Her sister was Dorothy Diemer Hendry (1918-2006). Her brothers were George Willis Diemer II (1920-1944) and John Irving Diemer (1920-1964).

Emma Lou received music composition degrees at the Yale School of Music (BM, 1949; MM, 1950) and the Eastman School of Music (Ph.D, 1960). She studied composition and piano on a Fulbright Scholarship at the RoyalConservatoire in Brussels, Belgium (1952-53) and at the Berkshire Music Center (summers 1954 and 1955).

She taught piano and organ at colleges in Missouri (Park, William Jewell, Kansas City Conservatory) in the 1950s and theory and composition at the University of Maryland (1965-70) and at the University of California, Santa Barbara (1971-1991).

She was composer-in-residence in the Arlington, VA schools under the Ford Foundation Young Composers Project (1959-61) and composer-in-residence with the Santa Barbara Symphony (1989-1991).

Honors have included a NEA fellowship in electronic music, a Friedheim/Kennedy Center award for her piano concerto, many commissions for chamber, orchestral, piano, organ, choral music. Her music has been published since 1957 and much of it is recorded. Her website is emmaloudiemermusic.com.